MONEY STORIES

Simple Ways to Help You Manage
and Invest Your Money

Mitch Fisher

BALBOA.
PRESS

A DIVISION OF HAY HOUSE

Balboa Press books may be ordered through booksellers or by contacting:

Balboa Press
A Division of Hay House
1663 Liberty Drive
Bloomington, IN 47403
www.balboapress.com
1 (877) 407-4847

Print information available on the last page.

ISBN: 978-1-9822-1087-8 (sc)
ISBN: 978-1-9822-1085-4 (hc)
ISBN: 978-1-9822-1086-1 (e)

Library of Congress Control Number: 2018910058

Balboa Press rev. date: 10/29/2018

CONTENTS

Spending and Saving

Investments

Insurance and Annuities

Real Estate

College

Retirement

Estate Planning

Advisors

ACKNOWLEDGMENTS

For my parents, Ri and Al, who encouraged me to do my best.

For my wife Karen, who loves me and shows me how to be more generous.

For my children Diane, Elliot, and Ryan, who make me proud and who improve our world.

For my children Jay and Carly, who gave me more reasons to live and to contribute.

For my brothers Larry, Bob, and Steve, who have made me happy all my life.

For my grandmother Jean, who reminded me to "count your blessings, not your troubles."

And for my mentors, John Wooden, Go-Go Gilbert, Stu Weissman, and Steve Fiore.

Without you, this book would not have been written.

PREFACE

In 1971, I sat in front of the Taj Mahal in India—because of a bet. It turned out that this experience was to be the catalyst for my career. That year, I was attending the University of Tel Aviv, taking a junior year abroad while at Claremont Men's College. Spring vacation was approaching, and students were making travel plans. The Middle East is truly in the center of the world, with many interesting neighbor countries and continents nearby. Many of my classmates had some cool travel ideas. "We're going to Amsterdam for a couple of weeks," said a few. "We're checking out the Greek islands," others said, or "We're going to Morocco and riding the Marrakesh Express."

I figured that my college friends and I had a good month to explore places rather than just settling for a two-week vacation. No tests would be given the first week we returned from spring break, and if we turned in our term papers early, before the vacation started, we could have an extended time of travel.

"Why don't we go someplace really spectacular, far away, like India and, say, check out the Taj Mahal?" I suggested. My friends laughed and showed me on the map that Agra, India, was three thousand miles away. "That's not too bad; I've hitchhiked to New York from LA in three days. Who wants to come along?" One friend said he was in. A bet was placed that we couldn't make it to the Taj Mahal in two weeks traveling overland.

Beginning with a flight to Istanbul, my friend and I traveled by train, truck, bus, and van through Turkey, Iran, Afghanistan, and

Pakistan, finally making it to India. On the banks of the Ganges River, we sat down on the grass in front of the amazing Taj Mahal, one of the Seven Wonders of the World. Built in 1632 by Moghul emperor Shah Jahan, it is the magnificent tomb made from translucent white marble to immortalize Jahan's favorite wife, Mumtaz Mahal. It was truly an "out of body" experience for me to be there. And it was day 13 since our journey had begun. We had won the bet.

I was able to see much more of India during that time. The Golden Temple in Amritsar and the Kulu Valley in Kashmir were two of my favorites. I even traveled in a truck over the base of the Himalayas to Kathmandu on this adventure. Although the accommodations were student hostels, cheap hotels, and sometimes a tent, we had no thought of ever turning back. Of course, many of these places are off-limits to most travelers today: the Khyber Pass, Kashmir, and most of Afghanistan and Iran.

I began my journey with $150 in my pocket and returned, about seven thousand land miles later, with $20. As a bonus, I collected the $5 bet from each of my two doubting pals. Thus, I had frugally spent about $4 a day on the trip of a lifetime. Sure, train rides in those days in the Middle East and Near East were a dollar or less. A bowl of rice and chicken was probably 25¢. That was a seemingly dumb wager on my part, filled with all kinds of failure potential, but it turned out to be an exciting expedition. No matter how you look at it, that was still pretty good money management for nearly a month.

It was also the adventure that began my career in helping others manage and invest their money.

INTRODUCTION

The first thing you should probably ask yourself about this book is: Who is this guy to be telling me about how to manage money? Fair enough. For starters, I am a multimillionaire but certainly not a billionaire. I have a home in Kauai on the beach, I have another home in the suburbs of Southern California, and I drive a new car, but I'm no George Soros or Oprah Winfrey. My clients are mostly everyday people: engineers, doctors, lawyers, rabbis, priests, business managers and executives, widows and widowers, teachers, and scientists. I have worked with many famous people too. You would probably know my clients who are Oscar award-winning actors and producers, film photographers, musicians, or artists who have paintings hanging in national museums. These clients have trusted me with many millions, and they have made many millions from my guidance. I won't claim to be the number one money manager of any group or in any financial survey. *Forbes* magazine has called me for comments because of my successful money management and to ask why my clients are loyal to me.

I suppose my bachelor's degree from the esteemed Claremont McKenna College and my being a certified financial planner (CFP) will carry some educational weight with you. I've earned my license as an insurance agent, real estate agent, stock broker, registered investment advisor, and corporate business owner during my career that started in 1974. These were tests of knowledge, sometimes difficult for me to pass. They were important educational tools but provided very little practical information about how to keep clients happy and to manage and grow money.

Most of all, I've learned the rules about successful money management from working in the field for so long. I've had great coaching lessons from John Wooden and Warren Buffett. When all is said and done, there's truly nothing better on a resume than real-life experience. The greatest compliment from clients that I've repeatedly received over time has been along the lines of "Since we've been working together, I don't worry about money anymore."

I would love to write you a great story like Jonathan Kellerman, J.K. Rowling, David Baldacci, Nora Ephron, or Harlan Coben…but these authors are in a league of their own. The best way I know to help lead you to a new kind of prosperity is to make my money ideas interesting and simple. As my favorite philosopher-poet, Ralph Waldo Emerson, once wrote: "To be simple is to be great."

So, let's get started.

LESSONS LEARNED

CHAPTER 1

ONE THING

CURLY. Do you know what the secret of life is? *Holds up one finger.* This.

MITCH. Your finger?

CURLY. One thing, just one thing. Stick to that one thing, and the rest doesn't matter.

MITCH. So, what's the one thing?

CURLY. That's for you to figure out.

These lines are from the movie *City Slickers*, with Jack Palance as Curly and Billy Crystal as Mitch. At one time or another we have all had friends and relatives, advisors and strangers, give us some words of advice. Some we remember and carry with us our entire lives. Most we forget in a moment. Some advice is valuable. Most of it is simply wrong or just baloney. My main job is offering financial advice to clients, family, and friends.

Surely you can remember something that stuck with you from a parent or grandparent. Here are a few words of wisdom that I grew up with: "A bird in the hand is worth two in the bush"; "Count your blessings, not your troubles"; "When the going gets tough, the tough get going"; "Keep your eye on the prize."

These phrases and little gems of insight gleaned from experience are important to us. They shape us and define us, especially when they turn out positively to provide us with strength, hope, or guidance. When it comes to money, the proven, time-tested words of advice are simple: "Buy low, sell high"; "Location, location, location"; "Build shelter against a rainy day"; "When investors are greedy, be fearful. When investors are fearful, be greedy"; "Never put off for tomorrow what you can do today"; "It's not how much you make that counts; it's how much you keep."

But is there just one thing? What do you think? If there was a verified formula for investing that produced a 10 percent proven return every year without fail, wouldn't most of us adopt it? If there was an unswerving, foolproof method for high yields, then you wouldn't need advisors like me. Is there one way to build a bridge, construct a home, carve a turkey, paint a picture, surf a wave? Not really. Investing is an art, not a science. Sorry, Curly, there just isn't one way to make money or keep it.

I had a relative who asked me the very same opening question at every family gathering: "What is the true meaning of life?" Sometimes I tried for a serious reply, and at other times I replied with a joke. After a variety of retorts went nowhere, I finally determined that the easiest way to answer was just to send the question back: "I don't know. What do you think?"

One day, as I was listening to the car radio, the Dalai Lama was appearing in town and being interviewed by a reporter. "So. tell us," the interviewer said to the Tibetan guru, "what is true the meaning of life?" My ears perked up. I cranked up the volume. *Oh boy, here we go. I'm not going to miss this answer. My relative will really have something coming from me at the next wedding or birthday party.* The Dalai Lama paused for a moment, then—and Mitch from *City Slickers* would love this—he said: "It's one thing. One word: contribution. If you contribute to people's happiness, you will find the true goal, the true meaning of life."

I have passed this bit of simple brilliance on to most of my friends and family. Unfortunately, I never had the chance to offer this truly insightful response to my inquisitive relative. She parted ways with the family through a divorce.

This book is my contribution to you. If these stories improve the quality of your life and bring you happiness when it comes to managing and investing your money…then my efforts will be worthwhile. I will be happy that I have contributed to your financial success.

CHAPTER 2

PERCEPTION

My three brothers and I go on a trip together each year to honor our father, who died of prostate cancer in 2001. We usually go scuba diving in a place like Belize or the Cayman Islands. We jump into some warm, clear ocean water and look at some undersea wildlife, play some cards, and catch up with each other and our families. One year, after the youngest of the four brothers finally became certified in scuba, we planned a dive at Tunnels Beach on the North Shore of Kauai.

Our newest diver was a little anxious on his first big adventure under water. He asked just about everyone he met on the island what it was like to dive at the place called Tunnels. One local resident told him: "Tunnels. Yeah, that's a great dive spot. Just watch out for all the sharks around there." Precisely what a new scuba diver wants to hear. Terror and trepidation filled the next few days. My brother considered not going on the dive, but we insisted he set his fears aside and suit up. Fortunately, we had the most wonderful dive master who knew exactly what to say and do. She simply and elegantly changed his perception about what was likely going to happen fifty feet down.

Once we arrived at the dive spot, the first question from my anxious brother diver was "What about the sharks out there?" The dive master responded, "Of course there are sharks out there. It's the Pacific Ocean.

I've been on one thousand dives, and I can tell you that sharks are like dogs. You have your Dobermans, golden retrievers, and poodles. The poodles are so mild and harmless, they barely have any teeth. They are cuddly and curious. There are plenty of golden retrievers out there that just want to swim around and have fun. The Dobermans are rare around here, and they really have no interest in you. We are not food to them. We are simply in the same ocean together, and if we don't bother them, they won't bother us." Ah, some simple and visual perspective, especially easy to relate to since all four brothers are dog lovers.

Our walk-in dive spot, Tunnels Beach, is located near the foot of the mountain range made famous in the movie *South Pacific*. It is commonly known as Bali Hai. In the movie, the words and melody of the song "Bali Hai" are so beautiful that, for most people, they make a musical imprint that lasts forever. We geared up with regulators and tanks, fins, and masks. As we began to wade into the exquisite water looking at the famous mountains, our dive master began to sing: "Bali Hai will whisper on the wind of the sea. 'Here am I, your special island. Come to me, come to me.'" She encouraged us to join in: "C'mon, you guys. Sing along with me. You know the song." We sang with her. It brought smiles to our faces and calmness to our demeanors.

What do you think happened next? About ten minutes into the dive, our dive master spotted a five-foot-long white-tipped reef shark with its tail poking out of a cave. She couldn't say it under water, but I'm sure that we all thought, *Hope it's a golden retriever.* She swam over and tickled the shark's tail. Out it came, circling us and checking us out, and then swam right back into the cave. The dive master motioned us closer and pointed at the tail. Each of us took turns touching and tickling the tail. When it came time for our new diver brother to swim up, you could see his eyes wide with wonder, not fear. He didn't look hesitant or nervous at all as he grabbed a bit of the shark's tail and gave it a wag.

What an amazing transformation! From having a heart-pounding fear of sharks for three days, he was now petting a wild white-tipped reef shark in a cave in the ocean. Just a few words and a song from the master changed everything.

So, when that fear comes along that relates to your money and investments, try to find some perspective.

CHAPTER 3

THE SKY IS FALLING

"I'm really worried about the market. I see on the news that we are going to have a crash."

This is a very common feeling among many clients. Even the most sophisticated and experienced investors will have moments of doubt and trepidation. Remember, a main agenda of the news people is to scare you. They want to grab your attention so that you will watch, listen, and subsequently be a part of their advertising audience. Advertisers pay their bills.

Rupert Murdoch, father of the modern tabloid and once head of News Corporation, is reputed to have said: "Given the choice of watching a young man escort an elderly woman through traffic across a street or watching the car crash on the opposite corner, people will always watch the car crash." In the movie *Up Close and Personal*, the TV producer played by Robert Redford says to his newscaster, played by Michelle Pfeiffer, "If it bleeds, it leads." It seems to be a natural tendency for most people to tune in to disaster.

Whenever clients are anxious or nervous about their money, I usually tell this story:

A man is pacing around the bedroom at night. His wife is trying to sleep, but his pacing is keeping her up. "What's the matter, honey?

Why don't you come to bed?" Her husband replies, "We have a loan due at the bank tomorrow, and we don't have the money for it." His wife gets the phone out and places a call. After identifying herself, she says, "Mr. Banker, I'm sorry to disturb you at night, but we have a loan due tomorrow from your bank, and we don't have the money to pay it." She hangs up the phone. Her husband says in disbelief, "Why in the world would you do that?" His wife replies calmly, "Well, now, honey, it's his problem. You can stop your pacing, and I can get some sleep."

As history has shown, patience with good investments pays well. It's rare if an investment grows and never falls back in price from time to time. It's true, of course, that century-old companies have failed and gone bankrupt. However, that's an infrequent occurrence. We have heard about the crash of 1929, which led to a Depression in the United States. We've had similar catastrophes more recently in the markets: the oil crises in the 1970s, the recession in the 1980s, the "tech wreck" in 2000, and the mortgage meltdown in 2008. Sometimes the news people get it right.

Many people who worry about bumps and depressions in their investments and sell them make their decisions too late. They seem to adopt the herd mentality and liquidate at the bottom when their nervousness finally takes over.

As markets rise and fall, it is best to stay calm and review your investments for their fundamental values and their exposure to volatility. The only formula we know that absolutely works in the world of investing is to buy low and sell high. So, keep the proper perspective, especially if the media proclaims that the sky is falling.

The week of my company's recent client appreciation event, the markets took a big slide. This is an elegant and fun party given to show our gratitude and "hug" our loyal clients and friends. Here's what I told 150 of our special clients and guests:

"Since the markets decided to pick this week, of all weeks, to pour some rain on us, let me take a moment to address the buzz before we have dinner and entertainment.

"Thank you to so many of you who were concerned that I was okay during this downpour. Not only was I okay, but frankly, I was rather ecstatic. I've been waiting for prices to come down for a long time, and this week they finally did. Everything was on sale! There was barely enough time to buy some good investments for all of you who wanted some. But I think we did. Remember Warren Buffett's favorite line, 'When investors are greedy, be fearful; when investors are fearful, be greedy.' So, what were most investors this week? Pretty fearful. So, we were being greedy.

"For you clients who've been with us long time, through the 1987 bank disaster with Mr. Keating, or the 2000 tech wreck, or the 2008 mortgage crisis, you already know that it doesn't pay to worry and to sell low. You know to turn down the 'noise' and the so-called media experts. You understand that good investments go up and down, and if you leave them alone, they usually grow nicely over time. You may have been concerned this week but not panicked. You know your investments will be back up again.

"New clients, welcome to some stormy surf. I can promise you that the ocean conditions will be glassy and calm again. The best that I can tell you is that we are being very careful with your cash. We use the coconut test I learned surfing in Hawaii. We throw the coconut in the ocean and we watch it—whether the current takes it right or left. We don't jump into high surf with both feet. We don't paddle out into big waves we can't ride.

"The economy is in great fundamental shape. Stay calm. Stay invested. Don't fight the fundamentals, and don't let the Chicken Littles and TV talking heads take you off course. If your account went up 20 percent last year and it fell back 5 percent like the S&P 500 this week, aren't you still 15 percent ahead?

"So, can we get to the food and the entertainment now?"

CHAPTER 4

ORGANIZATION

Like the rooms of many young kids, my room was usually a mess. There were clothes strewn everywhere, stuff on the floor—it looked like it had been tossed by burglars. Thanks to my mom, this disarray didn't last long. With four boys and a husband to care for, she was not about to be picking up after us. After several failed requests that I straighten things up and put my clothes in the laundry, she decided to take a different approach. She simply picked up my clothes and threw them in a bag and kept them hidden out of my sight. It wasn't long before I was out of underwear and socks. When I asked my mom about the missing clothing, she said, "If you don't put your things away where they belong, how will you find them?" My attitude soon changed about putting my things away. I've had the neatest rooms and closets ever since.

When it comes to finances, it can be easy to fall into being messy or disorganized. Unfortunately, there are more severe consequences than going sockless or "commando" for a day or two. You can damage your credit, lose important documents, or pay fines and penalties for being late. You can also waste a lot of time searching for information or worrying about money. Being properly organized and on top of your finances gives you more financial power and peace of mind.

One of my first investment clients would bring in a three-ring binder with him to our meeting. Everything was in tabs, three-hole-punched, and organized alphabetically. In response to any specific inquiry, the client would simply find the tab, open the section, and say, "Here it is. What would you like to know?" I'm still old school when it comes to recordkeeping, and I continue to use the three-ring binder for personal and business use. My Millennial and Gen X children tease me about it from time to time, and that's fine. This is the paperless digital age, so we can use the three-ring binder concept with our computer and smartphone by setting up a filing system and storing our data in the cloud.

As simple as it sounds, paying your bills on time is critical. Unless you are going to employ an outside bookkeeping service, you will be doing this yourself. There are many software applications for you to use to pay your bills in an organized fashion: QuickBooks is the standard today. I suggest making a list of all your regular bills, on paper or by spreadsheet, so that you can see easily how much you need to pay and which lenders, utility companies, and so forth have been paid month by month. You can establish an online direct payment from your financial institution, either manual or automatic. I recommend keeping your receipts by hard copy in an envelope by month or digitally. The rule of thumb for the IRS is that you hold on to all records for three years, but in some instances the IRS can go back as far as seven years for cost basis and expenses.

You should not allow anyone, except you or your bookkeeper, to have access to your accounts, distribute money, or pay your bills. I have one client who has told me, "I love to pay my bills before they are due, especially if I have the money!"

It takes discipline and commitment to become organized and to pay your bills on time. Like riding a bike, once you get the hang of it, you won't forget how to do it. Good organization will serve you well for the rest of your life.

Creating a monthly budget is important to having your financial "house" in good order. Budgets, income, and expenses are always changing, so expect constant fluctuations and remodels. Try not to cut things too close. Leave some room for emergencies and other unexpected expenses, and don't forget to put in a column for your taxes too.

You can organize your investments in the same manner. Set up a system listing your brokerage and bank accounts, real estate info, loan statements, insurance, etc. You can also include a separate file for transactions such as confirmations when you purchase or sell securities. Include a personal asset statement that lists your assets and liabilities. Update this statement every three to six months.

You should create a separate file for your estate documents. Your will, trust, powers of attorney, and real estate deeds, along with a letter of instructions, should be included in this file. Your attorney or financial advisor should have copies of these important documents.

In addition to these organizational techniques, it is critical to protect your personal identification in this twenty-first century. You can take many precautions in this area of guarding your ID, some simple and some sophisticated. There are companies that provide these protective services to keep your identity as safe as possible from hackers and predators. No system is foolproof, but it surely behooves you to take steps to lock your door and turn on the alarm when it comes to identity theft.

I've merely scratched the surface of financial organization in this chapter. The key is to get yourself organized now—and to stay organized.

To paraphrase French chef Alain Ducasse of the three-star Michelin restaurant the Dorchester: "there are many new and interesting ways at looking at ingredients".

There are also many ways to use new technology and different systems to organize your finances.

CHAPTER 5

COACH WOODEN

I was one of the luckiest kids in the world. I grew up around John R. Wooden. Coach Wooden was one of the wisest, one of the most caring, and certainly one of the most successful people who ever lived. He died a few months shy of one hundred years old, and his wisdom and legacy will live on forever. His Pyramid of Success is one of the finest teaching creations ever written. To me, he was like a second father, a teacher, and an inspiration for life. John Wooden was, in my eyes, the Dalai Lama of Western civilization. Most people know of him as the greatest college basketball coach of all time. I live and breathe his teachings every day.

Both of my parents went to UCLA in the 1940s. My father, an avid sports guy, loved the game of basketball. He was one of the first members of the Bruin Hoopsters, an alumni booster club for the UCLA sports programs. He personally welcomed Coach Wooden when the latter arrived from Indiana to Southern California to build a basketball program at my parents' alma mater. My dad and Coach Wooden became friends. They talked basketball and much more. They met often in a booth at Junior's Deli on Westwood Boulevard and talked for hours.

Coach Wooden was an extremely intellectual and learned man who loved literature (he wrote many books himself), religion, poetry, and philosophy. My father and I went to many of Coach's basketball practices in the stinky old men's gymnasium on the UCLA campus. We watched the practices and the drills and the plays. We were season ticket holders for half a century. Our seats were located two rows directly behind Coach Wooden, so we could watch him and his championship teams and hear just about every word he said. We might as well have been invited into the sideline huddle since we were so close to the action. In 1964, Wooden's UCLA team ran the table and won thirty games in a row to win the college basketball crown. It was the first of his record-setting ten NCAA basketball championships, and I was right there at all the games with my dad.

When I grew up and Coach Wooden retired, he and I became acquaintances. He had many people who would call him a friend. We would greet each other with a smile and shake hands at all the games. He had the warmest handshake I've ever known. I introduced my kids to Coach, and he always bent down to their level, smiled sweetly, and asked them, "Who is your favorite person?" or "What is the thing you like to do the most?" After he retired, he attended almost every one of the basketball games played at Pauley Pavilion, the arena at UCLA that he "built" when he recruited Lew Alcindor—Kareem Abdul-Jabbar—in 1965. I was with my dad at the Bruin Hoopsters' welcoming luncheon for Lew, and I received a smile and an autograph from the dynasty maker and the player whom many consider to be the greatest basketball player who has ever lived.

After he retired, Coach Wooden and his wife Nell had seats that were just a few over from ours. He was positioned a couple of rows up and on the end of an aisle, so that anyone who wanted to stop and say hello to him could do so easily. I used to love to introduce clients and friends to Coach Wooden. He would sign autographs and talk for a few minutes with us. The lines to meet him became longer and longer as the years went by and his teachings and success became legendary.

Some considered him a saint or a great philosopher along with being a fantastic coach. He had tremendous values and left nothing to chance, monitoring every detail of his endeavors. He was famous for starting out his first practice with a lesson on how to properly put on and tie laces of a basketball sneaker. He would sit his team down in a circle and ask them to remove their shoes and socks. Although the players scoffed and shook their heads, he explained that if the sock was not tight around the foot, or if the shoe was not laced in the proper way, then blisters might occur that could affect an athlete's performance. At his practices, I witnessed a relentless repetition of the basics: moving your feet quickly, holding your arms a certain way, positioning your body advantageously, etc. No team could match the fundamentals and the endurance his players developed by doing these exercises.

I have used these fundamentals of efficiency, positioning, and endurance in my world of managing money. My clients, knowingly or unknowingly, owe a good part of their success and our relationship to John R. Wooden.

I never heard Coach Wooden use the word *win*, although that's pretty much all he did. He was known to have never uttered a profane word, and his angriest phrase was "goodness gracious, sakes alive." Many people don't know this, but he rarely coached strategy during the games. He had prepared his team to the max, and they knew all the plays and the players, so Coach let his assistant coaches take care of many game-time decisions. It seemed to me, sitting so close, that the main focus of Coach Wooden during the games was to hover over and yell at the officials for that extra competitive edge. He constantly pointed out to the referees if an opposing player was pushing or holding or if a ref had missed something favorable to his Bruin team. He would call out the official by his first name: "Come on, Joe, look at number

14. He's holding our player by the waist. Gracious sakes alive, Joe, call the foul. Don't let him get away with it."

When my father passed away, Coach Wooden wrote me and my family a beautiful handwritten letter about the friendship and support that the two of them shared. Of course, he ended with a line from one of his favorite poems: "If death should beckon me with outstretched hand and whisper softly of an unknown land, I shall not be afraid to go, although the path I do not know."

CHAPTER 6

DO IT NOW

Each of us has a different perspective about time. If you've been in a near-death situation or lost a loved one, you may appreciate the value of time a bit more than someone else. Those who punch in and out of work on a clock, or production people meeting deadlines, will have a different feel and definition of time. For businesses and professionals, it's probably the phrase "time is money."

It can be very difficult to focus each day on our best interests when we are faced with interruptions, disturbances, and distractions. Ben Franklin created a daily scorecard to stay on track with his goals and accomplishments.

I use two simple techniques to stay focused. These have worked beautifully to allow me to get the most out of each day. The first is to make a list of items to address and accomplish and then prioritize these items. The second is an overriding mantra: "Do it now!"

Sometimes there are only eight or ten items on the daily list, and sometimes there have been as many as seventy-five. It's a source of pride and joy for me to be able to check off each item and see how many things I've gotten done in one day. I have kept and filed my daily to-do list for as long as I can recall. There are occasions when I've made a note or jotted down a phone number or a name on the daily list and then retrieved this information later. The list also becomes the predecessor and starting point of the next day's list. I transfer most of the items that weren't finished the previous day to the new list.

You can prioritize the important daily items in many ways. *H*, *M*, and *L* can be designations for high, medium, or low priority, respectively, placed next to each item. Colors like red for urgency or the phrase "must do" can be incorporated. Some list makers prefer to use a number scale, such as 1 for the most important item, 2 for the item of second priority, and so on. I like to put a circle next to the most critical items, so they stand out, and then place a check in the circle when each one is completed.

Time managers may vary in their advice about what to tackle first. Like answering questions on an important exam, you may want to knock off the easiest items first, then go back and tackle the tougher ones. I prefer the opposite approach: attack the most difficult things first, then cruise through the easy items. Approaching the end of the day, if my list is 70 percent check-marked, I feel good. If it's not, I may just try to check a few more off before putting the list away.

I'm not sure if I took "Do It Now" from a person or a book. It most likely had its origins in personal experiences that led to a hypersensitivity to the value of time. It's not complicated at all. If something needs to be done or is requested, you just get to it right away if you can. If the light bulb goes out in the bathroom, then go get a new one right away and put it in. When the phone rings, pick it up. If the flowers are drooping, water them now or pull them out. The tickets are on sale? Buy them now. You snooze, you lose.

In my firm, we have a rule to get back to our clients within twenty-four hours. We respond in a like manner: If it's a phone call, we call back. If it's a letter or email, we write back. I say to our clients, "If you haven't heard from me in twenty-four hours, either I'm dead or I didn't get the message." This attention to service is just in our DNA, and our clients love it. It is a huge reason for our success. People want responsiveness, and we give it to them as promptly as we can, every day.

Following one new client meeting, I needed to answer a question that required a little research. As soon as the couple left my office, I went straight to the computer, found the answer, and emailed it to the clients. A few minutes later they called me. "We received your email and the information just a few minutes ago. Thanks. Did you say you always respond in twenty-four hours or twenty-four minutes?"

In my opinion, procrastination usually doesn't pay. With caller ID and texting today, it's easy to ignore someone. Shopping on the internet provides so many choices that you can be overwhelmed and worn out, which may lead you to give up and do nothing. No matter how long it takes to decide, or how much research and thought is invested, you are going to make choices that do not work out. No one gets it right every time, so be willing to make your mistakes and move on. Surely, big decisions require time and thought, weighing the pros and cons, taking your time to do it right.

For most daily decisions, however, applying the "Do It Now" mantra should work well. Ralph Waldo Emerson wrote, "Nothing is more simple than greatness. Indeed, to be simple is to be great."

Benjamin Franklin had a daily list with a morning question: "What good shall I do this day?" In the evening before Ben went to sleep he asked himself: "What good have I done today?"

CHAPTER 7

GOLF AND BUSINESS

Many times, I've heard these words of advice from my dad: "Take up golf. All the big business deals are made on the golf course." It wasn't until age fifty-seven that I took up this sport. The game of golf came to me in a fortuitous way.

We had a great mail carrier, Steve Fiore, in our neighborhood. When he and I first met, he asked me, "Did you go to Inglewood High School?"

"Yes, I did."

"Well, I went to your rival, Morningside High, and you and I played against each other in sports. Are you still playing?"

"Yes, basketball is still my sport, and I'm playing three times a week."

"How about golf?" he asked.

"Nope, not ready for that just yet," I told him.

Fast-forward fifteen years or so, and he asked me one day if I was still playing basketball regularly. "No, I had to quit recently. The knees are wobbly and sore, plus the younger guys are driving by me like I'm stuck to the floor." The next day I found a golf putter on my doorstep with a note from Steve: "If you want to learn the game of golf, I'll be happy to teach you." Fortunately, I took him up on it, but he had some terms and conditions.

First, he would not accept any payment from me for lessons. We were friends. Second, I would do it his way only. Third, I would not play on a full-length eighteen-hole golf course for six months. I agreed to his rules on one condition: that I could pay him back by introducing him to my friends and playing with them on their private golf club courses. We had a deal.

He gave me a book on golf. It had big pictures and a few descriptions of each phase of the game. "Read this first." Next, he gave me a used set of golf clubs and told me, "We will be going to the driving range for a while." We went every week for three months. He coached me patiently in the fundamentals of golf. Once he could see that my swing was smooth and balanced and my ball-striking was on point, he said, "Now we'll pitch and putt for a while. In golf, you need a good short game."

For the next three months we went to several small courses each week that were about twenty-five hundred yards long. (The average full-length golf course is around sixty-five hundred yards long.) No driver club was needed on most holes. These courses were designed for the short game, primarily two hundred yards or less from tee to hole. Steve was teaching me accuracy and club control, not distance. Putting was a big focus on these pitch 'n' putt courses. As the saying goes, "Drive for show; putt for dough."

Along the way, Steve was schooling me in the correct body position and teaching me the proper club to use in a variety of situations. He taught me how to hit a low ball from under a tree limb. He showed me how to accelerate the club through the sand in a bunker. He schooled me in using an eight iron to bump and run when just off the green.

He also was teaching me the rules and the etiquette of golf. You don't walk through someone's putting line, you must stand far enough away from the other player to be out of his or her peripheral vision, and you must make sure that you pull the cart up past the green as a courtesy to oncoming players. There was a lot more to this game than a jump shot and a quick first-step drive to the hoop.

Finally, the six months was up, and I was ready to hit the big links. I arranged with one of my country club friends to play at his private golf course. Steve was happy to be playing on a beautifully manicured golf course for members and their friends only. He was anxious for my debut, just as a good teacher would be anxious for his student to shine in the real world outside the classroom.

On the third hole, I hit my drive in the fairway, but my second shot went into a greenside bunker. As I stepped into the sand, Steve's training was clearly in my head: put the ball on your front foot, dig in a little for balance, pick a spot two inches behind the ball, open the club face, and swing all the way through with the club. The ball popped out of the trap, onto the green, and landed two inches from the hole.

Our host said, "Hey, if Fisher is going to be scaring birdies from the sand on his first outing, I want some lessons from you too, Steve."

Coach Steve has my lifelong gratitude for introducing me to the game of golf in the very best of ways. He gave me the fundamentals and made me practice them over and over until they were right.

The same can be said about investing: learn the fundamentals first and follow them, and they will serve you well in your financial life. Fundamentals are vital to success.

About two years later, I was getting ready to tee off at the Wailua golf course on the island of Kauai. This is usually rated as one of the best one hundred public courses in the USA. A fellow came up next to me at the first tee and asked if he could join me. As we walked and talked and whacked the balls around next to the amazing ocean views and swaying palms, we found that we had lot in common.

We really liked each other. He told me that he was in Hawaii on a holiday with his girlfriend who was a physician in Phoenix. He said that our meeting was fortuitous because his girlfriend had been telling him how unhappy she was with her financial advisor. Two weeks later, I returned to the mainland and met with them in our Southern California office. They had driven in from Phoenix to meet me, visit with our staff, and open their accounts.

It took a while, but ultimately, my dad's golf suggestion proved to be valuable. A good client had come to me through the game of golf.

CHAPTER 8

NINE PROMISES FOR INVESTMENT HAPPINESS

Adding the word *Investment* to the Nine Promises for Happiness from Coach Wooden, here are my simple promises you can adopt for success:

1. I promise to diversify and balance my investments and not to put too many eggs in one basket.
2. I promise to be patient and hold on to good investments during occasional market storms.
3. I promise to try to buy low and sell high.
4. I promise to be wary about paying too much in taxes and never to let the tax tail wag the investment dog.
5. I promise to save money and spend money, and to find ways to enjoy a balance of both.
6. I promise to do my homework before investing, not to rely on investment tips, and to hire professionals who can give me good counsel and work in my best interest.
7. I promise to be prepared financially for emergencies and life-changing events with proper insurance and estate planning.

8. I promise to be open to taking risks within my level of tolerance, because if nothing is risked, then nothing can be gained.

9. I promise to remind myself that there is really no such thing as financial security in life. Instead, it is my own peace of mind that comes from knowing I have done my best to invest wisely.

CHAPTER 9

BEN FRANKLIN
ON MAKING DECISIONS

We have decisions to make each day of our lives. Some decisions are easy and trivial; some are big and important. Since we cannot make the best or the right decision all the time, it is important to figure out a way of making choices that serve us best. Procrastinating, making no decision at all, is the same as deciding on a plan. "If you don't know what to do, make the decision that hurts you the least" was a technique used by one of my clients.

I prefer to use the Benjamin Franklin method for making decisions. Ever since the day I learned it, I have used it and encouraged others to adopt it. It is so simple and so powerful.

Benjamin Franklin was one of our most admired Americans. Whenever he had an important decision to make, he would take out a piece of paper and draw a line down the middle. On the left side, he would write down the pros, or the reasons for moving ahead. On the right side, he would write down the cons, or the reasons not to go forward. Then, he would add up each column. Simply put, if there were more pros than cons, he would say yes to the decision and carry on.

"You may delay, but time will not, and lost time is never found again," wrote Benjamin Franklin.

Here's Ben expounding on his decision-making methodology:

> My way is to divide half a sheet of paper by a line into two columns; writing over the one "Pro" and over the other "Con." Then during three or four days' consideration, I put down under the different heads short hints of the different motives, that at different time occur to me, for or against the measure. When I have thus got them altogether in one view, I endeavor to estimate their respective weights; and where I find two, one on each side, that seem equal, I strike them both out. If I judge some two reasons con equal to some three reasons pro, I strike out five; and thus proceeding, I find where the balance lies; and if after a day or two of further consideration, nothing new that is of importance occurs on either side, I come to a determination accordingly.

In addition to listing the pros and cons, it may be important to give each item a degree of priority or an order of significance. You may want to attach a numerical weight to each piece of the decision or make your own point system to measure each element. No matter how you do it, this easy way to focus and to resolve should become a part of your decision-making process.

One last Ben Franklin quote to nail the point: "Never leave that till tomorrow that you can do today."

MEDIA
AND POLITICS

CHAPTER 10

POLITICS AND THE TWILIGHT ZONE

For many years, I conducted financial seminars to attract new clients. One question I liked to pose for audience participation was "Do you know the rules of the game when it comes to politics?" These rules are implicit in what follows:

Question 1: What do politicians fear the most? Answer: Not being reelected.

Question 2: What do politicians need if they are to be reelected? Answer: Votes.

Question 3: What do politicians need to acquire votes? Answer: Money.

Question 4: Who gives the politicians the most money? Answer: Wealthy individuals, special interest groups, and businesses.

Question 5: What do these main groups of contributors receive in return? Answer: Political influence and favors.

Question 6: What are these favors? Answer: Mostly tax breaks.

Few people would disagree with this oversimplified view of our political system. There are so many examples that it would take up the rest of this book to state even the main ones.

There are approximately 2,600 pages in the United States Federal Income Tax Code, and it takes a whopping 75,000 pages to explain the code. (According to the Tax Foundation newsletter, there are exactly 2,652 pages in the United States Tax Code with slightly more than 1,000,000 words.) By way of comparison, the King James Version of the Bible has 788,280 words, *War and Peace* is 560,000 words, and the *Harry Potter* series is just over 1,000,000 words. Do you think perhaps there have been some businesses and special interest groups who have contributed to these pages?

We have our own basic rules of the game with our clients. There is no place for politics, sex, or religion in our business relationship. How we manage your money has nothing to do with how we vote.

Many investors use the political environment as a consideration for their financial planning. We surely have our share of hawks and doves, Republicans and Democrats, conservatives and liberals. It is important to determine if you may have a bias, for instance, of not making investments with companies that might sell weapons or tobacco. Many companies have been discovered to mistreat their employees or be unethical in their operations. Some investors want to buy only US companies, and others may want to be socially responsible in their purchases.

These are legitimate concerns and client preferences that must be part of any proper financial plan. Room must be made for a person's political standpoint if one is to construct a proper and inclusive portfolio. The emotional side of an investor cannot be ignored and must be an integral part of money management. Today's ESG (environmental, social, and governance) investing, impact investing, and green investing are not trends, but rather permanent forms of investment philosophy.

Is your personal disposition prone to bringing politics into your financial planning? If it is, there are many ways to satisfy your desire to be politically proactive with your investments.

In the end, it is not the job of the financial advisor to try to dissuade you from ignoring your political preferences. In fact, it is critical for your financial advisor to listen to your considerations and see them as important and to build a financial plan that incorporates your emotional side as well as your logical side. It should be a collaboration of forces: your sensitivity, your preferences, your risk tolerance, and your practicality. These play directly into your desired peace of mind, which is huge part of your overall financial plan.

Politicians can make and change the laws surrounding investments. The 1970s was an especially great time to make money for small businesses and professionals. Doctors, lawyers, actors, producers, writers, and small businesspeople were able to stash unlimited amounts of cash in their defined benefit pension plans. They would make contributions, legally allocate a high percentage for themselves over their employees and receive a tax deduction from the federal government. Some of these high earners would then borrow the funds by way of a "friendly" credit union. In a nutshell, the retirement plans were great tax shelters that gave one full use of the money. One day, Congress said "enough," closed the loopholes, and changed the rules. They put limits on the amount of contributions and stopped the credit union turnstile system.

Although politics certainly stirs the investment pot from time to time, political events and politicians come and go. In my view for the long-term investor, politics really plays a minor role. It is far more important to look at the basic economics and management of any investment before including it in your portfolio.

With apologies to our political clients, when I am asked about politics during our financial meetings, my response is pretty standard: "My personal political views should not be part of our discussion. The most I will say is that politicians are like babies' diapers; they need to be changed often—and for the same reason."

I was exposed to politicians very early in life. My dad was a small businessman, and he found it advantageous for his business and personally satisfying to help elect his choice of senator or congressperson. As youngsters, my brothers and I walked and drove around with our dad, putting posters up in the neighborhoods. There were many politicians at our home for gatherings, discussions, and events.

I will share one very memorable evening at a political fund-raiser in our home. The creator of the *Twilight Zone*, Rod Serling, was there. My father asked Rod if he wouldn't mind telling us, his four young boys, a bedtime story. He was happy to do it. Tucked cozily in our beds, listening to Rod's story in that famous TV tone, my brothers and I were enchanted, in our own personal twilight zones. It was surely a once-in-a-lifetime experience.

CHAPTER 11

MEDIA PUNDITS, EXPERTS, AND PROGNOSTICATORS

We live in an era of instant information: stock market quotes in real time on your smartphone, and television stations dedicated to money talk. Along with the data, charts, interviews, news, and market updates should come extreme caution regarding background and intent.

Let's remember the way things work in the media business. First, we must remind ourselves of who pays the media for their content and commentary; it's the advertisers. They want "eyeballs on the screen" and will pay more for greater exposure. Second, the media knows that "if it bleeds, it leads," so they are driven to deliver excitement and disaster. Third, to get you to watch and keep watching, the drama must be front and center. "Breaking news" is the exclamation of the media.

The author Harry Dent, a self-appointed expert in demographics and stock market analysis, has written several best-selling "guidebooks" about the future of your money. In my opinion, he has provided his sensibly sounding point of view without getting his predictions anywhere close to reality most of the time. In his 1999 book *The Roaring 2000s*, Harry described a Dow index that would likely reach 35,000 by the year 2003. The Dow went the other way for many years and has never been close to this level. Harry reversed course in 2012, when he predicted the S&P 500 Index would soon lose 30 to 50 percent. Not long after his negative prediction, the S&P 500 Index took off on a growth pattern that eventually reached an all-time high.

Of course, there have been some very accurate prognosticators and economists along the way. Elaine Garzarelli, working as a stock analyst at Shearson Lehman, predicted the exact day of the 1987 Black Monday stock market crash. She became the darling of the financial world, but to my knowledge, her crystal ball has filled with clouds ever since. Alan Greenspan, the former Federal Reserve Board chairman, was ahead of the curve and accurately suggested that "irrational exuberance" in the markets would lead to a downturn. He was right on the money, and the dot-com craziness in the late 1990s led to a collapse of the stock market.

The best fortune-teller of them all was baseball's Yogi Berra, who once said, "I don't make predictions, especially about the future."

Investing for the long run can be simple if you are able to tune out the noise and the hype of the media all around you. Make good investment choices, hold on to them through the tough times, trim the laggards, balance and diversify your portfolio, and select a culture of good management. These are the foundational blocks of making money over time.

You might absorb this type of simplicity from one of my favorite movies, *Being There.* This film starred Peter Sellers as the dimwitted Chauncy (Chance) Gardener. One day, Chauncy meets the President of the United States in the library of wealthy donor Benjamin Rand. Here's the conversation:

> President: Mr. Gardener, do you agree with Ben, or do you think that we can stimulate growth through temporary incentives?

Chance the Gardener: As long as the roots are not severed, all is well in the garden.

President: In the garden?

Chance the Gardener: Yes, in the garden. Growth has its seasons. First comes spring and summer, but then we have fall and winter. Then we get spring again.

President: Spring and summer?

Chance the Gardener: Yes.

President: Then fall and winter?

Chance the Gardener: Yes.

Benjamin Rand: I think what our insightful friend is saying is that we welcome the inevitable seasons of nature, but we're upset with the season in our economy.

Chance the Gardener: Yes, there will be growth in the spring.

President: Hmm, well, Mr. Gardener, I must admit, that is one of the most refreshing and optimistic statements I've heard in a very long time. I admire your good solid sense. That's precisely what we lack on Capitol Hill.

CHAPTER 12

POLITICS AND INVESTMENTS

When I was twenty-one, I went to work for a US congressman in Washington, DC, for a summer. It was a memorable experience. In 1971, there was an enormous amount of political energy oozing out of every corner of our nation's capital. I rode the underground railway daily and sat beside the leaders of our country: Senators Ted Kennedy and Thomas Eagleton, Speaker of the House Carl Albert, and House Minority Speaker and soon-to-be president Gerald Ford. There wasn't much security in those days. During that year, there was a major legislative debate in Congress to approve the right to vote for eighteen-year-olds. It seemed obvious to me, and to most of the country, that if you could fight in a war for your country, you should have the right to elect your political representatives. This Twenty-Sixth Amendment to our Constitution was overwhelmingly ratified with a vote of 94–0 in the Senate and 401–19 in the House of Representatives. The legal age to vote was officially changed from twenty-one to eighteen.

While in Washington DC, I learned first hand that politicians wield great power. In the long run, however, politics and politicians have very little effect on the course of financial markets. During election years, the positions of the candidates when it comes to the health-care, energy, financial, and real estate sectors, to name a few, can temporarily affect the stock or bond prices of companies across the world. For instance, if an important politician declares that more restrictions should apply to the approval or availability of drugs, then the pharmaceutical companies feel the sting. Sometimes these political declarations and, ultimately, the regulations can destroy a company or hurt an industry. Usually, these political maneuverings are short-lived and merely cause minor changes in the financial markets. Strong companies with good management will change with the politics of the day and keep on going. Interest rates and corporate earnings are the real drivers of our economy and the market prices. It's good old Economics 101—supply and demand—not politics.

If a powerful politician makes it known that he or she wants to continue tax breaks for the solar industry, or that he or she supports oil exploration in certain areas, the value of solar companies or energy companies can slide or soar. In the short term, investors with good information and a sense of the future can profit from the pronouncements of politicians. In the long run, the laws of supply and demand take over. If a product or service proves beneficial for users and purchasers, it won't matter what the politicians think or say about it.

There have been numerous studies devoted to the political parties in power and their effect on the financial markets. US presidents have been viewed as being good or bad when it comes to the economy. If a president serves during a time when there is no war or during a technology boom, and the markets have great success, is it because of activities generated in the Oval Office?

In my opinion, it rarely matters who is in political power; the markets will do what they do whether the leaders are Republicans or Democrats. Politics can play a role occasionally, but simply good investments will pay dividends in the long run.

SPENDING
AND SAVING

CHAPTER 13

ROCK AND ROLL LIVING LARGE

In the seventies, I worked for a pension and profit-sharing administration company. Whenever a business owner, athlete, entertainer, writer, physician, or other professional made lots of money, that individual's accountant would usually send him or her to our firm. My job was usually to design and set up a retirement plan with the highest tax deduction to give most of the benefits to the owners and key people.

In those days, there were very few limits on the amount of contribution and the legal method of favoring the highest-paid people. I was fortunate to be able to assist the rich and famous, and their advisors, with terrific techniques to legitimately sock away hefty funds for their retirement and save them considerable taxes along the way.

Sometimes these retirement plans would be severely abused. The contribution was tax-deductible because ostensibly the money was being set aside for future retirement purposes. However, those who had these plans were allowed loans from them. You could contribute a significant amount, with almost no upper limit, deduct the contribution from your taxes, and turn right around and borrow the money back for personal and current use.

The closure of this "loan game" loophole began with a crackdown on a credit union scheme for dentists in San Diego. The method was to contribute the highest amount to your retirement plan, take a tax deduction, then head on over to the credit union set up for this purpose and borrow it all with no penalty. When the IRS caught wind of these arrangements, they closed the loophole and established a maximum loan amount of $50,000. In addition, all loans beyond this maximum would have to be repaid within twelve months of the new rule or else the outstanding balances would be fully taxable. Ouch!

Many entrepreneurs and professionals had borrowed millions of dollars from their retirement plans to use personally and in the present. You might imagine that some people had reinvested the money in real estate and their businesses, but many of the loans were simply spent to serve a lifestyle. And the funds that were needed to repay the accounts under the new government regulations were just not there anymore.

One day, I was asked to go out to Westlake Village near Los Angeles to meet with a member of a successful rock-and-roll band and have him sign some papers related to the new regulations. He was the lead singer for a group that had scored three gold records with their first three albums. He was also the trustee of their retirement account. As I drove through this wealthy suburb, I admired the large homes with the beautiful landscaping. Arriving at the given address, I was surprised to see a brown lawn with droopy plants and peeling paint on the house. It was certainly the sore thumb in a lovely neighborhood.

I knocked on the door. The lead singer opened it and asked me to come inside. The expansive home was entirely void of any furnishings. It was completely empty except for a guitar and an amplifier, the latter used as the singer's only available seat. I could hardly believe my eyes. Here was the leader of one of the hottest bands in the world with a big house, a brown lawn, and not a stick of furniture anywhere. He signed the paperwork to pull out the little cash remaining, pay off his loans and close his retirement account.

"What happened to you?" I asked him.

"Oh. You know us rock-and-rollers," he said. "We like to live large and don't care too much about tomorrow. We just spent it all. Thanks for coming over."

CHAPTER 14

LOTTERY WINNERS

Several lottery winners have become clients of mine over the years. These lucky new millionaires I served were very different in personality, age, and lifestyle. They all had one important financial objective in common: to make the money last for a lifetime. They hired me with this goal in mind.

David Baldacci wrote a book called *The Winner*. It's about a guy who was able to fix the lottery by secretly adding weight to the numbered flying Ping-Pong balls. With the extra weight applied, the thief knew in advance which balls would be the winners. The thief would buy a ticket, arrange the weight of the Ping-Pong balls to coincide with the ticket number, and select a stranger who would follow his instructions if given the chance to become very rich. After collecting the prize, the stranger would have to leave the country for a few years and turn the money over to the thief. The stranger would live in luxury and travel the world. The thief would disburse some of the winnings to the stranger and keep the rest for himself. Without spoiling the ending for you, I'll just say that the detective was able to track down the crook by unveiling a pattern of lottery winners: most winners had blown through their money in a few years, but a few were living extremely well and had their money managed successfully.

Each one of my lottery clients, although the winning dollar amounts were different, had been through the same spending process before we met. First, they had paid off their bills. Second, they had taken a trip, purchased a new car, or bought some clothes or jewelry. In other words, they spent some of the money on themselves after being free and clear of debt. Third, they had fixed up their homes. None of them had bought a bigger or fancier house. Fourth, they had given away some of their fortune to family and friends who may have needed it or may have simply deserved a gift of kindness.

After spending and giving, they realized it was time for preserving. Fortunately, they came to me with plenty of time to invest their winnings and make them last a lifetime. We calculated their life expectancies, created an annual income budget, and estimated a conservative return on the money. Using this planning and meeting our projections, they would have all the money they needed to live in comfort, with a very healthy amount left over to leave to their heirs.

One of the lucky lottery winners who used our service was a man in his seventies. For years, he had gone down to the local market each week and bought a group of ten tickets. He liked certain numbers and combinations that he felt had significance for him. He would come home, spread the tickets on the kitchen table, and sit down next to his wife in his lounge chair to watch TV and await the announcement of the winning numbers.

Then the lucky day arrived, and he hit the jackpot. He kept one-third for himself and his wife. He set aside the other two-thirds for each of his two children. Sadly, he died about six months after his big win, so he only enjoyed his fortune for a short time.

For him, I think it was more about picking the winning numbers and seeing them light up the TV screen. Oh, and his family is surely set for life.

CHAPTER 15

SISTER AND BROTHER

How can two people born from the same parents be so completely different? If you can answer that question, there's probably a place for you in the world of genetics or psychoanalysis.

I invested money for a kindhearted, soft-spoken gentleman from England who had a daughter and a son. His two children could not have been more different than Dr. Jekyll and Mr. Hyde. The daughter was lovely, caring, smart, hardworking, and sensible. The son lived in a very poor area, rarely worked, and was inconsiderate and troubled. When their father died, they split up the inheritance in equal parts, but that was the end of any resemblance of equality.

The inherited funds passed through a living trust and protected the son and daughter from probate delays and attorneys' fees. However, there was no provision for staging the distributions, preserving any capital, or considering the inequality of the children.

Almost as soon as the son received his money, a relatively significant amount, he had blown through it. He bought unnecessary consumer goods, gave money to his buddies who begged or scammed him, and went on wild binges that might embarrass a rock-and-roll star.

The daughter was quite the opposite. She paid off some debts, adding a few things to her wardrobe and her home, and then told me:

"That's it. Invest the money for my future. I can live within my budget, in a home that I like, and take a few trips. I'll be fine."

No doubt, you know the ending to this story line: the son is likely on the street somewhere, and the daughter has turned out to be happy and successful, adopting a child of her own and traveling the world. She has a sizable nest egg to provide for her daughter's college education and has enough to travel and live well for a lifetime.

Her father would be extremely proud of her today.

CHAPTER 16

TOO FRUGAL

If you think about it, there is an unlimited supply of money out there. Governments can print more currency or borrow from others. There is really no cap on what a person can make, especially in the United States. Yet, for some people, this adage applies: "You can never be too thin or too rich."

It doesn't matter how much money you might have, there is an undeniable emotional position and attachment to the way you spend or save it.

I believe there should be a balance of spending and saving. For simplicity and visual aid, I used to draw two circles on a piece of paper and say, "There are basically two types of people when it comes to money. In the first circle, you have the ones who make money and then save anything that is left over. In the second circle, you have the people who save some of their money first and then spend what is left over. Do you know the difference between these two types of people?" Then I would draw an arrow from the second circle to the first and say, "The ones in this circle who save first and spend what is left over usually employ the ones in the other circle."

Enjoying the pleasures and comforts of what money can buy and saving for the future and a rainy day can be tough to balance. There is simply no way to avoid addressing our own financial balances when it comes to saving and spending. The extremes, overspending or being too frugal, can play havoc on your peace of mind. In my view, it is okay to treat yourself to something special or important from time to time, even though it may go against your fiscal disposition.

If you need a holiday, a getaway, then find a way to take one—within your budget. If you want to redecorate your home and it means a lot to you, then create a budget and do it. Your old car is not making it anymore? Then say goodbye, trade it in, and spend a little more for some new wheels.

These types of expenditures are usually not going to be life-changing financial decisions. Large purchases or big, long-term commitments are the ones that can hurt you. A little compulsive buying should be fine now and then but think deeply and carefully about significant expenditures.

I have some extremely conservative clients. It doesn't matter how much money they have, they find it very difficult to spend it. This fiscal tightness could be from a deeply embedded feeling of fear, probably generated from childhood. Perhaps their family or friends lost their business or their home. Maybe a tragedy occurred in their life that they connected to money, or perhaps they were brought up in a place in which every penny was watched and accounted for by their parents.

One wealthy client told me once, "I was at the market the other day and I thought to buy two avocadoes, but the voice in my head from my father told me that I should only buy one."

That's just being too frugal.

CHAPTER 17

PLANNING PAYS

Fortunately, I have been able to serve clients from almost every profession and background: engineers, doctors, teachers, attorneys, actors, producers, photographers, artists, directors, scientists, writers, rabbis, priests, business owners, et al. The primary attributes they have in common are being smart and using their talents to become successful. They didn't arrive at their success by accident. They used their passion and persistence to become great.

This story is about an all-around great couple. Loving and devoted parents, she skillfully and carefully managed the family finances while he was entertaining people all over the world. He was an outstanding sportsman and the winner of several Guinness Book of World records. His achievements were for joggling. What, you've never heard of joggling? Well, joggling is a competitive sport that combines juggling with running using any set of three or more objects. Passion and talent are what led my friend and client into a very successful entertainment business.

We first met when he was already engaging people at corporate parties and appearing on *The Tonight Show*. He and his wife were bringing up two young girls and saving furiously for their college. Education was a very big deal in their home, along with sports. He and his wife were very athletic. He especially enjoyed extreme sports and big sporting events. I took him to a UCLA basketball game at Pauley Pavilion and said hello to Coach Wooden. Our relationship was pretty much cemented for life after that experience.

Through the prosperous years and some belt-tightening financial times, this couple saved money religiously for their children's college and for their own future. They socked away as much tax-preferential money as they could in their IRAs, especially since he did not have a company 401(k) or pension plan. They paid down the principal on their mortgage each month, and within fifteen years they owned their home free and clear. They hadn't even reached the age of forty-five. One day they told me, "Our girls are just about finished with college with just a couple more years of tuition payments to go. We were wondering if it was possible to retire early, instead of waiting until we reach sixty-five."

We looked at their assets together. Even though their house was paid off, we did not use their home equity as part of our calculation. You need a place to live, so we left that asset outside of the income projections. We added up the funds in their retirement accounts, family trust, and other real estate. We projected the value of these assets with a reasonable rate of growth until their age sixty. Then, we added the annual contributions to their IRAs plus interest to this total. With this future total value of their overall assets to be used for their retirement, along with their anticipated monthly social security, we were ready to make some assumptions and calculations.

We began with an assumed growth rate of a little less than their actual ten-year return they had experienced in their accounts. This was a real number, not just a guess. We applied an annual cost of living and inflation percentage increase to the projection. Things usually cost more down the road. Then, we presumed a net percentage to be paid in income and capital gains taxes.

Now we were ready to ask, "How long will my money last?" After some discussion about their anticipated monthly needs for a comfortable retirement, including a hefty allocation for travel and fun, we arrived at a monthly dollar amount. We plugged in this modest income number and we looked at the bottom-line results.

Kaboom. An explosion of amazement and relief went off in the room. In this retirement scenario, their increasing monthly income lasted well beyond their projected ages of one hundred, and there was still an enormous inheritance left for their daughters! They were amazed at the income and the surplus. They started to tear up with joy and relief.

"What would happen if we increased the monthly income?" he asked.

So, we doubled the amount of their projected monthly income. The numbers showed us once again that their money would last well beyond the age of one hundred. The only difference was less of an inheritance for the girls. Just for fun, we doubled their projected monthly amount again and lowered the assumed growth percentage rate. Surprise. Their money still lasted a lifetime, and there was simply less of a substantial estate left for the kids. Their faces lit up with enormous joy. Thirty years of scrimping and saving and paying down their debts, and now they were free!

She said, "This is incredible. I had no idea we could retire this way. We are so grateful."

He said, "I'm absolutely floored, and I think we are in shock. I have chills. We thought you were going to say that we would have to save more money now and cut back our expenses. This is truly amazing. We have enough to last us forever, and the girls will be set for life. I'm going to cry."

I gave him the box of Kleenex and sat back to enjoy the glow that was coming from them.

Planning and saving pays.

CHAPTER 18

COSTLY HABITS, PETS, AND HOBBIES

Race cars, racehorses, birds, boats, and storing stuff can be expensive. Money is surely there for us to spend, but sometimes our pastimes and passions are over the top. Before you know it, your hobby or pleasure can land you in a "money pit" and make it very tough for you to dig out.

If you earn enough, and if you can enjoy the fruits of your income and savings, then grab a hold of your desires and appreciate them. If the financial burdens begin to weigh on you or your enthusiasm has waned, then try to get out sooner rather than later.

We have lots of clients who love animals: horses, dogs, birds, and fish. One woman fell in love with racehorses and began buying them for the joy of stroking them and watching them run. She hoped that they would win her some money racing and that her equestrian affections would pay off handsomely. As she continued to add to her stable of thoroughbreds, her income and savings became less and less enough to pay for their care and training. Her racehorses won occasionally, but not nearly as often as needed to support their ownership. Of course, this woman's emotional attachment to each of her thoroughbreds became stronger over time. They were her children, and the thought of selling any of them and parting ways was just too much for her to consider. Eventually, reality set in and she was forced to let go of many of her fine horses, mostly at a deeply discounted price and a loss to her. "I knew that they were draining me financially, but I couldn't let go. I'm not sorry I owned all of my horses, but I just should have said goodbye to some of them sooner."

Another common story I hear is about the cost of care and medical treatment from our pet owners. Today's treatment of cancer and arthritis, implanting of bionic body parts, etc., has become a major part of veterinary care and profit. Chemotherapy, steroids, knee replacements, and other treatments are expensive and oftentimes unnecessary or unreasonable. My wife and I have owned springer spaniels and loved them from birth to death. They have been part of our family with their own unique personalities, minds, and moods.

As with our human friends and families, we should be responsible to provide comfort and treatment if our pets are sick. However, there usually comes a time when the cost and treatment will not really protect and preserve their quality of life. I have watched uncomfortably as pet owners have cut deeply into their investment and retirement accounts to add a few months to the lives of their animals. I admire and understand their devotion and care; however, practicality and sensibility should dictate a clear course of action sooner rather than later. I've learned that strong emotions will usually overcome any financial concerns or considerations, and it is not my place to argue with love and devotion.

Many of our clients are car aficionados and surely have enough money to enjoy the thrills of owning and racing fast cars or showing off classic vehicles. For many, they enjoy the adrenaline created by speed. For others, they take pride in driving, restoring, or owning a beautiful automobile. Jay Leno and Jerry Seinfeld have warehouses of fine cars. No doubt, these guys can easily afford their car hobbies and collections. Some of the automotive purchases are for investment, to enjoy a car for a while and then sell it, hopefully at a profit. Unfortunately for some car lovers, the storage and upkeep can be a serious drag on finances. J. P. Morgan once said, "If you have to ask how much it costs, you can't afford it."

Have you ever looked around your closet, attic, basement, or storage facility and asked yourself, "Why am I keeping all this stuff?" If you're thinking that you'll wear it again, you'll use it later, or your kids will want it someday, think again. If these things are stuffing up your rooms, that's only a problem of space and clutter. If you are paying for these things to be stored, that's another matter. We have a client with three storage facilities. She is on a budget and providing housing and security for a bunch of things she doesn't even know she has and that she will never use again. It's tough to get her to go clear her things out, consolidate, and save some money. Since old furniture, paintings, appliances, and clothes will likely wind up in a thrift store in the end, we encourage you to go with an objective friend or relative and have him or her help you sort out and give your unneeded or unwanted stuff away now.

You can receive a tax deduction for these contributions to charity, and someone else may be able to use the items. As the comic once said, "You can't take your stuff with you. I've never seen a U-Haul trailer hitched to a hearse."

CHAPTER 19

SOMETIMES YOU JUST TREAT YOURSELF TO A POOL

Sick and tired of the LA traffic and congestion, our client moved to Arizona. She owned a couple of rental properties that gave her income, plus she had social security and a pension from her job. She wasn't rich, but she was comfortable—at least until the desert heat arrived every summer.

Single, with children and grandchildren, she had a good income and a modest lifestyle. She had been frugal her entire life, so it was a long time coming and difficult for her to make this call to me.

"Mitch, I need some money now to fix my yard and to get a pool here. I can't stand the heat. I don't go out, I don't buy stuff, and I live an easy life, but I've got to cool off. Do I have enough money to landscape my yard and put in a pool?"

This is a part of my work that I really enjoy. It's not as if she needed my permission. It was her money. It was her life. She had savings and retirement assets. She simply wanted someone who knew her, and knew her circumstances, to say, "It's okay to spend your money on yourself." She needed some positive and practical reassurance that she wouldn't run out of money someday by putting in a pool.

In her case, it wasn't an easy answer. She would be withdrawing a significant portion of her savings in cash to complete her project. The several conservative calculations I used to project her finances forward showed that her money would last just a little past her life expectancy.

"Well, I'm going to die from this heat a lot sooner if I can't cool off. If I live too long, then my kids will just have to help out and give me a little extra love and comfort."

They say life is short and that we must live for today. They also say that we must put money away for our future and save for a rainy day. It's crucial in financial planning to try to balance these two rivers of thought and emotion. In her case, she was terribly unhappy and uncomfortable. She had enough money to last a very long time. It was time to take the plunge.

So, I told her to treat herself to the pool and said we would do everything we could do together to make her money last for a long, long time. She screamed, "Oh thank you, thank you!" I could feel her through the phone jumping up and down for joy.

Of course, she already had an estimate in hand and a tentative construction date. She agreed to let me help with the contracting and the payments, to be sure that no money changed hands with the contractor until each phase of the work was completed properly and to her satisfaction. She watched the contractor's every move just like a hawk in the desert sky. This was one of the few times I can recall that a construction project was brought in right on time and precisely on budget.

When it was all done, she called me from her backyard. "Thank you for everything. If it wasn't for you, I wouldn't have this." And the next sounds I heard were splashing water and a lot of wonderful laughter.

INVESTMENTS

CHAPTER 20

DON'T BE SHOCKED

Janis Joplin, Jimi Hendrix, the Doors. The Hollywood Bowl in Los Angeles was a great venue for these performers in the 1960s. As a kid growing up in LA, I was able to see many of the great rock-and-roll icons before they died.

I'll never forget some unusually excited fans in the audience wading through the water in the moat in front of the stage to try to touch Jimi Hendrix during his set. When some of the dripping-wet fans made it on to the stage, Jimi unplugged his electric guitar and stopped the concert: "If you won't leave the stage, we'll all be electrocuted," he said. Then he calmly walked off until the water was mopped up. I'm pretty sure they did away with the moat soon after that Hendrix concert.

You can easily be shocked with hot stock tips or bad investments. So, in most cases, stop the "sure bet" concert before you get electrocuted. On many occasions, I've heard this refrain: "My friend told me about this new company. According to him, this stock is really going to take off soon. Can you buy me some?"

Certainly, we have seen a meteoric rise in many fine companies. Some very fortunate investors have become very rich by investing early in new and up-and-coming companies that go on to change our worlds and grow exponentially. These enterprising owners and investors took the risk and reaped the rewards. However, my experience has shown that whereas some of these stock tips occasionally pay off, rarely do most live up to the hype.

Usually the tips are too late or have faulty information associated with them. The get-rich-quick lure just doesn't pan out most of the time. Caveat emptor—buyer beware.

When clients ask about new companies or "tips," I run these companies through our financial "MRI" screening and try to determine if they have true value and potential for growth. Since new companies will generally have little or no track record, the fundamental investment elements will not be present. The important statistics of profit margins, revenue growth, debt equity, price earnings, and price-to-book ratios (to name a few) are tough to determine without decent longevity. It's difficult to grade a new company, in teacher's words, on a curve.

Therefore, this is my usual response to an inquiry about a stock tip: "From my perspective, this investment has no intrinsic value. It is likely to fall, as most do, and to disappoint you. It could even become worthless. Are you prepared to lose some or all your money by investing in this company? If your answer is yes, then let's go ahead and buy some shares, so if it does go up, you will be in the game and you won't be left out. If your answer is no, then I suggest that you pass."

By using this simple guide to "striking it rich" with stock tips, you may avoid being shocked or even electrocuted by bad investments.

CHAPTER 21

KISS

In 1974, I was very fortunate to be hired by Dennis Gilbert. Known as Go-Go Gilbert for his energy and enthusiasm, Dennis is the consummate promoter. He began his career with a large insurance company, built a terrific team of salespeople in the 1970s, and then became one of the top sports agents of all time. He was simply the best I've ever known at making you feel comfortable the moment you met him and then later becoming your friend. He wrote the first of several record-breaking contracts with Major League Baseball for his client Barry Bonds. Dennis went on to represent some of the most successful sports and entertainment people in the world. He is also the proud creator of the Professional Baseball Scouts Foundation.

One of Go-Go's favorite questions was "Do you believe in the KISS method? You know, keep it simple stupid." (I've since changed that to "keep it simple and sincere.") There is something special and rewarding about breaking down a complex idea and making it easy to understand. Dennis was truly a master at simplifying the benefits, getting to the heart of the matter, and motivating people to make a positive decision.

When you are looking at a financial product or service, it behooves you to try to understand the basics. Let's look at analyzing a company stock that might appear complicated but that can be broken down into some essential parts for easier understanding.

If it was suggested to you, or if you were driven on your own, to buy shares in XYZ Inc., then there should be many good reasons. How can you determine if a company has value and/or potential for growth? There are so many places to go for a determination: financial statements, analyst reports, charts, graphs, key statistics, ratios, and formulas. Insider information is illegal, but public data about a company is easily obtainable. We are surely in an era of transparency.

The first inquiries should be: What does the company do, who are their main customers, and what is the competition? What products or services do they offer? No doubt, you have seen clever advertisements on billboards, on TV or the internet that grab your attention but give you no idea as to what is being offered.

The next questions should be about the management of XYZ Inc. Who is running the company, what is their experience, what is their expertise, what is their success pattern, and what are they paying themselves? Good management can make a company consistently profitable, whereas bad management can destroy a company. You can research the main people at a company by looking into their backgrounds, success patterns, and philosophies for growth.

Financials and fundamentals are also at the center of making a good decision. Key ratios and statistics can provide valuable historical data, like looking through the rear-view mirror. They can offer a profile, a pattern, and a somewhat recent look at the company's relative value. I have a simple point system to use for analyzing a company's stock. The points include profit margins, current price with highs and lows, debt, cash, price-to-earnings ratio, price-to-book ratio, price-to-sales ratio, corporate governance, quarterly growth and earnings, dividends, and management pay. These fundamental financial elements can never guarantee the growth of an investment, but they are very good clues for potential success.

Always remember that investing is an art, not a science. If someone were able to create a tried-and-true guaranteed formula for success, then there would be a lot of financial people out of work. If the great Warren Buffett can lose 30 percent in a year (he did), so can anyone. Even with the vast information and investing tools of the internet, you cannot simply plug in a formula for making 10 percent per year and watch it unfold consistently every time. Take it from Warren, "Investing is simple, but not easy."

Keeping things simple should serve you well before you put your money into an investment. Viewing the basics will not always produce positive results, but these fundamentals are a good place to start.

My aunt used to have a common retort when asked about many things in her life: "It's complicated," she would say. Investing doesn't have to be complicated. Imagine yourself up in a helicopter, hovering above the trees, rather than being in the middle of the forest looking for a way out. It's always better to review an investment from above and look over the fundamentals before you put real money into it. Use the KISS method; it should serve you well.

CHAPTER 22

EGGS

Rockwell International, a huge manufacturing conglomerate, spun off their semiconductor division, Conexant Systems, in 1999. As a former Rockwell employee, my client received approximately ten thousand shares of Conexant stock, which was trading around $90 per share—about $900,000. Fortunately, these shares were held in a tax-deferred retirement account.

These shares represented a significant portion of my client's retirement assets. The company had prospered and grown substantially over the previous years while he had been employed there. A loyal and conservative engineer, my client did not want to make any changes, believing that Conexant would continue its strong growth. Since he was "inside" the company, he felt he would also have his finger on the pulse of any important happenings. He had become relatively secure with the growth of this stock and did not want to part ways with any shares.

It took several meetings and in-depth discussions about diversification to convince him otherwise. My recommendations were to trade in a large portion of the stock over several months and add other growth investment sectors. "I know," he said, "you shouldn't keep all your eggs in one basket, but this company has been so good for me, I just can't see selling the stock."

After much emotional struggle with the idea of letting go of the stock in the company that had made him "rich," he ultimately took the advice. We began to diversify. The first month, we liquidated two thousand shares at $90. The stock began to fall. The next month, we liquidated another one thousand shares at $85. The stock fell some more. The next month we traded in an additional one thousand shares at $80. By the fourth month or so, he had one thousand shares remaining in his account, at a price of $70. The value of his previously held Conexant shares had now been reduced by $200,000 to a total of $700,000.

Fortunately, two important aspects had come into play. First, he was able to completely avoid any taxes on the sales of Conexant. Taxes could have been sizable because he had received the stock at an extremely low price. However, since the shares were held in a retirement account, there were no capital gains taxes to pay on any of the liquidated shares.

Second, we had used the proceeds of the stock sales to diversify into other areas, such as financial services, health care, technology, and real estate. These sectors had gone up in value rather than falling rapidly, like the stock price of Conexant.

Sometimes a similar story ends with making a big mistake. A person might be better off by hanging on to a great investment instead of selling it to diversify. In most cases, however, it is truly better to have a wide range of investments for someone with a long-term horizon and a conservative risk.

Several years later, when this client's account balance had doubled with the new diversified holdings, we looked back together at the decision. The $90 stock price for Conexant was now $3 per share.

CHAPTER 23

HARD TO BELIEVE

A woman approached me after one of my investment and asset protection seminars. In a very low voice, she asked if she could meet with me soon about one million dollars that she had in her bed mattress at home. "Say that again, please," I said. I thought either that she was crazy or something fishy was going on. I had heard a lot of stories before, but this one was unimaginable. Why would anyone store money like that in a mattress?

True to my nature of wanting to believe people, plus my added curiosity, I was willing to give her the benefit of the doubt. Since she'd asked to come to my office, I'd only be out a little time to find out the details. Whether that time would be a loss or would result in a gain remained to be seen. I was intrigued to hear her story. It turns out that some things, as hard as they may seem to believe, truly are stranger than fiction.

The woman was from Vietnam and married to an American. Her husband, a real estate developer, had recently passed away. Because he'd been a general partner in several struggling or failing properties, he was being sued by his real estate partners to recover some of the losses. She was a part of the proceedings that had just recently settled. Her financial exposure was minimal because most of their assets had been tied to the real estate partnerships. When she attended my seminar, her husband's creditors were just a few days away from signing an agreement that would release her from any further monetary risk or responsibility. For this reason, she had one million dollars in her mattress.

As a survivor of the war in Vietnam, and with politics aside, she had received two large checks from the US government as part of a reparations plan. She did not want to cash these checks for fear that the creditors would be hesitant to complete the settlement on the table if they knew there were more assets to chase and possibly recover. Legally, she had been told that these reparation payments were her separate property and not subject to the claims of her husband's creditors. No matter. She wanted to wait until the settlement papers were signed before going to the bank and depositing these government checks worth nearly one million dollars. Can you blame her?

In the end, the settlement went through. She waited a few weeks for the smoke to clear. Then she made her appointment with me, added her deposits, and we began our investment relationship together.

CHAPTER 24

BOLT AND BUFFETT

Ask three financial advisors to tell you the best investment plan, and you'll probably get four opinions. It's like asking "Who is the best actor?" or "Who is the best guitar player?" or "Who is the best poet?" These are subjective "bests" and are determined by someone's opinion.

During the 2016 Olympics in Rio, sprinter Usain Bolt proved for a third straight time, against his peers and measured by the clock, that he was the fastest man alive. There is nothing subjective about his position in the world of human speed. It is strictly objective, and there is no doubt or discussion about it. The world watched as he ran the fastest, time and time again.

Unfortunately, we do not have an objective method for becoming the best investor, but we do have several ways to train and race for the best results. The Sage of Omaha, Warren Buffett, has outperformed the S&P 500 Index and beaten his competition repeatedly. How does he do it?

Here are a few of Warren's investment principles: (1) Invest in companies with a high owner's stake. "We like to eat our own cooking." (2) Avoid companies that frequently dilute shares to raise money. (3) Invest in debt-free or low-debt companies. (4) Ignore daily stock price movements and focus on business performance. Short-term price changes are meaningless if there are good long-term expectations. (5) Choose companies run by honest and competent management. (6) Buy low and sell high, and if a company is doing well, keep the stock.

I would add diversification to this list of how to win the investing race. Diversifying your investments is more akin to a marathon than it is to an all-out sprint by Usain Bolt. As an example, the investors who lost big in the "tech wreck" of 2000 were overloaded with IPOs and technology companies. If you have money invested for growth across a wide range of investments, both in style (large, medium, and small caps) and sector (health care, technology, financial, real estate, consumer goods, industrials, materials, energy, etc.), you will likely be rewarded with consistent returns.

CHAPTER 25

SURFING

Surfing has always held a special place for me. Growing up in Southern California with the Pacific Ocean nearby and loving sports, I found that surfing was a natural magnet. My mom loved the sand and sea. She used to take me and my three brothers when we were toddlers down to the beach. She managed to unfold two big "playpens" to keep us corralled where we were sometimes able to nap. She taught us to swim in the beautiful Pacific Ocean.

At eleven years old, I had my first surf lesson at Manhattan Beach. At twelve, I had my own surfboard, used and dinged up but thrilling to ride. A year later, my friends and I were being dropped off at the beach—two of us carrying two ten-foot boards, one under each arm— to catch the waves until we were completely exhausted.

It was teenage heaven in the 1960s. The Beach Boys from nearby Hawthorne were cranking out the surf tunes. Sandra Dee was Gidget on the beach in the movie, and Sally Field as Gidget was turning heads at Malibu Beach on TV. I could hardly wait to wax up the board at the crack of dawn and paddle out into the glassy swells. In those days, there weren't that many surfers in the water, so there were plenty of waves to ride. Unfortunately, I was never very good at this sport, but I really loved it, and the passion I had for it was deep.

Family and business ultimately put surfing much lower on my life's priority list. Our vacations were often to Hawaii or a beachside venue where I could jump in the waves for a little while. Eventually, my knees went south, and so did my surfing days. It's tough to make any headway through a wave on a board when you can't really bend your knees. Today, I still enjoy the waves by bodyboarding with fins or bodysurfing. If there's a heaven, I hope they have waves to ride there.

One memorable surf trip I made in midlife was to Cabo San Lucas in Mexico with ten guys. They were younger and more talented than me, and much more passionate about surfing than just about anyone I had ever met. We rented a house along the Sea of Cortez and surfed until we could barely move our arms. While it was still dark in the morning, we would head out in our van on a bumpy dirt road, to be in the surf when the sun came up. It was a bit chilly and somewhat eerie, but it was an exquisite thing to watch the sunrise from the ocean while sitting on a surfboard. After two or three hours, we would go to breakfast, followed by another surf session until about noon. Then we would head for home, have lunch, and take a nap. When we awoke in the afternoon, we would watch film from that morning of us surfing the waves. We had a retired surfer dad along with us who was our photographer. For our last hurrah each day, we would paddle out in the late afternoon and ride until sunset. This was a surf trip to remember.

Here's how surfing relates to money management. Surfing is unpredictable and fluid. It moves like money moves, in patterns. It can be charted and watched, but it may never be counted on to act the same way.

In sports like football, basketball, or soccer, the field is turf, the court is wood, and the goal is in a fixed position. In skiing or snowboarding, the mountain doesn't move. In surfing, however, each wave is different. Waves move fast or slow. They can be big or small, and break in a different way each time. There is an ocean current that can be weak or strong. Waves can break close to the shore or a long way out. Underneath the waves, there is sand or rocks or coral, and the bottom can be deep or shallow. There are infinite shapes, sizes, and movements of waves, just as there are innumerable events that shape the financial markets. For a surfer, there is the thrill of the ride and the fear of the wipeout. For the investor, there is the thrill of a great profit and the disappointment and possible wipeout of making a very bad investment.

In Hawaii, I learned about the coconut test. Before any good surfer paddles out, he or she gauges the surf. One easy way to learn about the direction and strength of the ocean current is to toss a coconut into the water and watch where it goes and how fast it travels. With investing and financial planning, you can employ the "coconut test" by doing your research, employing good advisors, and thinking about your move before you jump into the surf with both feet and paddle out.

CHAPTER 26

BIG BETS

Some people consider life to be one wager followed by another. Investors who trade regularly are betting on the short term. The sports industry has become a multibillion-dollar dominator in large part because people simply love to bet on the outcome of games. Las Vegas was built in the desert sand not even a hundred years ago. Need we go any further? It's important to realize that betting has a place, "no risk, no gain", but measuring your own risk tolerance is critical to financial success. If you swing for the fences, you often strike out. Most people can curb their appetite to bet big. Others just can't help themselves.

Here are a few of my favorite betting stories that made history. The complete accuracy of these stories cannot be verified, except for the personal story at the end:

- Calvin Coolidge, a president of few words, was so famous for saying little that a White House dinner guest made a bet that she could get the president to say more than two words. She told the president of her wager. His reply: "You lose."

- In 1936, Art Rooney won $160,000 at Saratoga Race Course. With his winnings he formed the Pittsburgh Steelers, one of the most recognizable and profitable professional sports organizations in the United States.

- John Lennon and Elton John were together in the recording studio. Elton said later, "We worked on 'Whatever Gets You Thru the Night.' I said, 'If it reaches number one, you [John Lennon] must play onstage with me.' After its US release in 1974, the song hit number one on the Billboard charts." Lennon fulfilled his end of the bet on Thanksgiving Day by joining Elton John on stage at Madison Square Garden as a surprise guest. This was Lennon's last major performance.

- Golfer Phil Mickelson placed a $20,000 bet on the Baltimore Ravens to win the 2001 Super Bowl. The odds were 28–1. "I liked their off-season player acquisitions," Phil said. Much to everyone's surprise (except for the clairvoyant Mickelson), the Ravens ended up defeating the New York Giants, 34–7, in Super Bowl XXXV. Mickelson took home $560,000.

- Stephen Hawking is known as one of the great astrophysicists of the twentieth century. He placed high-profile bets as a sort of insurance policy against his own discoveries. He made the first wager with physicist Kip Thorne concerning the existence of black holes. Hawking bet Thorne in 1975 that the well-known x-ray source known as Cygnus X-1 did not harbor a black hole; Thorne disagreed. After evidence mounted that the system truly had a black hole, Hawking finally conceded the bet in 1990, giving Thorne his "prize," a subscription to a popular porn magazine—much to the consternation of Thorne's wife.

- Lucy Ricardo had trouble at the candy factory, but Warren Buffett had a vision in 1972 that was sweeter than anyone could have expected. Buffett bought See's, a previously family-owned candy company with stores around the American West. Founded in 1921, the business became one of Buffett's favorite investments. For an outlay of $25 million, his return has been more than $1.35 billion. This acquisition turned a sweet profit for Buffett with the company where Lucille Ball trained for her classic *I Love Lucy* candy factory comedy episode.

- In 2007, Pete Rose finally confessed to the worst-kept secret in Major League Baseball: he was betting on his team's games. But what people probably didn't see was the full extent of his gambling problems. "I bet on my team to win every night because I love my team, I believe in my team," Rose said. When the Reds lost, Rose wasn't just feeling the agony of defeat; he was also feeling the agony of deplete in his wallet. If that wasn't bad enough, his gambling led to his lifetime ban from the sport and from entrance into the Baseball Hall of Fame.

Finally, here is a true story from my annual get-together with several friends and members of our Claremont College championship basketball team. (They insisted at our last gathering to be mentioned in this book.) Please indulge me for a moment or two and read these true words written by my Stag teammates Rick Reed, John McKniff, Jerry Groff, and Don Lewis. These verses describe a bet on a putt and are engraved on a trophy plaque in my office:

The Putt

As legend has it, one Brent "Herbal" Hanson, bon vivant, world traveler, and raconteur extraordinaire, once deemed it wise to wager on the single swing of a golf club. The wager proposed by Hanson was dinner for life if this putt was true. The Wagerer figured the fix was in and that the odds were clearly in his favor. He sized up the probabilities and made the bet. The Wagerer's confidence was obscene; no one, professional or gifted amateur, had a ghost of a chance of sinking this putt. It was extremely long, and the two-tiered green undulated, rocked, and really rolled.

Indeed, the putt was so difficult and failure so certain that the Wagerer demanded nothing in return. Nothing. Confidence spilled out of his pores. But this was to be a moment in space and time when Providence and coincidence would align in a magical cosmic convergence.

As the assembled Claremont Stags looked on in anticipation, Mitchell "the Fish" Fisher addressed the ball. Then, in a hyperfocused visualization, he backed away from the ball and looked things over from every angle and possible line. He sighted down the line, and he sighted up the line. The Fish assessed the wind, slope, and speed again and again.

The intensity of the Fish's concentration was palpable. Then, with a firm wrist and a steady eye, the Fish stroked the ball. As the ball briskly moved over the rippled terrain, the suspense gripping the Stags became unbearable. Dinner for life was on the line, and destiny itself was focused on each revolution of the ball as it moved inexorably toward the cup. Finally, with a quiet *kerplop*, it was all over. Miraculously, the putt was nestled in the bottom of the cup.

All the Stags, save one, howled in astonishment and appreciation. The Fish danced and shouted his way around the green, high-fiving the tribe in triumph and jubilation. The sound of the Stag celebration reverberated into the surrounding hills and canyons; javelinas, deadly serpents, and mountain lions scurried for cover as the sonic boom moved up and down the canyons in waves.

The solitary figure who did not share in this historic moment of joy was the utterly discombobulated Mr. Hanson, a man quite literally struck dumb by the putt. Unfortunately, his condition, despite the passage of time, has not dissipated. The Wagerer remains a man in deep disequilibrium, the singularity of the event having burned every trace of that day from the deep gray ridges and tissues of his brain. It is said that Mr. Hanson now suffers from Norman Bates syndrome. He harbors a memory so horrific to him that clinical repression provides his only solace. The Wagerer is a man adrift in the fog of repudiation.

So, dear Stags, another year has passed and we must now lift our glasses once more to the Fish and the putt. While dinner for life has evolved into dinner once a year, let both the spirit of the wager and the brilliance of the putt continue to live long in our hearts.

And while we gather annually to celebrate, among many other blessings, the Fish and the putt, let us pray that over the years the Wagerer will come to acknowledge, and indeed come to celebrate, the simple fact that faith was rewarded on that fateful fall day and that history has permanently put its stamp on the putt.

CHAPTER 27

FOCUS – THE ACTOR

A very fine actor I know traded in his lines and the camera for being a full-time dad. He put on a pair of boots, worked on his ranch, and raised his kids. He also did some stock trading part time and learned a lot about finances and what moves securities. One day he looked around, saw that his children were grown up, and decided to return to acting. He was so good that very soon after he came back to the big screen, he was nominated for an Academy Award. In the same year, two of the films he starred in were nominated for Oscars. He had a thrilling dilemma: "At which Academy Awards nominations table should I sit?"

Before he returned to acting full time, he wanted to continue stock trading with an analytical system developed by a friend. After discussing his goals and his desire to keep his hands busy with his day trading, he and I decided together on a simple compartmental investment system. He would have three investment "drawers": one for his personal stock trading, one for his real estate endeavors with his trusted realtor, and one for his long-term investments with me. This has worked beautifully and successfully for many years, except for one bump in the road in the early part of our relationship.

His growth stocks and equity funds with our advisory service were taking a little dip soon after we began our business relationship. Nobody likes to see their assets lose even a little ground, but nothing goes up all the time. One day he said to me, "We need to get into some fixed income. Bonds have some real upside potential, and it's time to make a move out of the growth sectors." Of course, I asked him to remember that the daily ins and outs of trading were to be handled as we agreed via his personal trading account and that the long-term investments were my assignment. Back and forth we went on the merits of his securities, market timing, and the possibilities for bonds to have their day in the sun.

Finally, it was the obvious that proved most persuasive. I said, "You are on top of the world in your career. You are acting in great films, working with the best scripts and the finest directors, and making lots of money. Do you really have a need for bonds and a fixed income in your long-term growth plan? You surely don't need to generate any more income now. Why move your nest egg and retirement dollars out of good growth stocks and funds into a fixed-income style that doesn't connect to you and to your financial goals? Why don't you focus on what you know and what you do best, filmmaking? Let me focus on managing and investing your money so it will grow steadily over time."

So, we cleared that up and agreed on the obvious: fixed income meant fixed income, and growth meant growth. He went back to making movies, and I continued making long-term equity investments for his account. In the decade following our conversation, his long-term investments averaged more than 16 percent annually, while the fixed-income style would have barely earned him a 2 percent annual return.

We've both been very happy that we were able to bring the obvious into focus and agree on the best course for growth in the long run.

INSURANCE
AND ANNUITIES

CHAPTER 28

INSURANCE IS INSURANCE

There will probably be many insurance people angry with me when they read this chapter, but I can write these opinions because I've probably been in their shoes. I was a former full-time insurance agent.

In May of 1974, I returned to the United States from abroad and began looking for my career path. I made a list of things I wanted in my work, such as an unlimited income, a strong industry, a long-lasting product, limited travel, and the opportunity to help people. It turned out that these prerequisites led me to mostly sales jobs. People didn't call them marketing or consulting positions back in the day. After interviewing with several businesses, including Caterpillar, where the position was for tractor sales (not exactly the right fit for a city guy from LA), I wound up in front of a few insurance sales managers who were hiring agents.

The one I liked the most, Dennis Gilbert, had a warm manner, a good sense of humor, and an aura of success around him. I knew that he would be a great coach from the moment we met. As silly as they seem today, some of the first words he said to me were "You can only do three things in life: you can be a guru in the sand and play all day, you can go to work for 'the company' and maybe get lucky and marry the boss's daughter, or you can be in business for yourself." I joined the

Prudential Life Insurance Company that year and began selling life insurance door to door, campus to campus, office to office.

Life insurance is a great product that can provide cash, security, and peace of mind. That's why it's been around for two-hundred-plus years. Parents purchased it from me for family security, law students obtained it to pay off loans, businesspeople bought it to protect their interests, and retirement plans paid for it because it could provide extra tax benefits. Life insurance serves a primary purpose: to protect against an economic loss in the event of death. In my opinion, it does not provide a decent investment return.

Essentially there are two types of life insurance: term and permanent. Term insurance is easy to understand. It terminates. You are "renting" your insurance for a period of years, paying the premium during that time, and then when the term is up, your coverage ends. Permanent insurance offers a cash value or savings element to your policy. This type of life insurance is like a home mortgage in which part of the payment goes to interest and part goes to the principal. These permanent policies have different names, including whole life, universal life, indexed life, and adjustable life.

With the permanent insurance policy, part of your premium goes to the cost of the death benefit, and the other portion goes to savings or cash value. You can borrow from the existing cash value in a permanent life policy in the same way you might borrow from your real estate by using a home equity line of credit.

The primary advantage of the permanent life insurance policy is that your coverage can stay in place (it is permanent) beyond any term period—if you continue paying the premiums at a level that sustains the policy. In other words, you are buying the policy, not renting it.

Because the cost of insurance increases with the person's age, it is difficult for any savings or investment portion of a policy to keep pace with this escalating drag on potential growth. This mortality or insurance cost is like a boat with a big net of fish trailing behind it in the water. It is harder to make the boat go fast and move along with the drag of the fish-filled net. The older you become, the more fish there are in the net.

Oftentimes, these permanent policies are sold as retirement supplements. I was once a proponent of this idea. However, I long ago abandoned this method, and I have yet to see any of our clients use their life insurance policies as a regular source of income at retirement. Sure, you can borrow a stream of income on a tax-free basis, and it sounds great, but you are simply making a loan of your own money and restricting or reducing the death benefits along the way.

Sometimes, these permanent or cash-value policies can provide an important source of equity. Bing Crosby was able to purchase the racetrack in Del Mar by borrowing from his life insurance policy.

Most equity or bond fund investments have their own impediments to growth: fees, commissions, administration expenses, etc. These are generally much lower than the increasing mortality and expense costs of carrying a life insurance death benefit, especially at older ages.

If you have a permanent "need" for life insurance, not a temporary one, then I recommend that you choose the least expensive permanent cash-value policy, assume a reasonable rate of return, and make that purchase.

If you only intend to keep life insurance until your children are grown, or until your home is paid off, or to ensure your business debts, key employees, or partners are protected, then choose a term policy.

Most term policies have a conversion privilege, meaning that one can obtain a permanent policy with the same company without having to qualify or take a medical exam. Should you become sick or hurt and you don't want your coverage to lapse at the end of the term, you could most likely convert your term policy to a permanent policy, keep the benefits in place, and pay a higher premium.

This area of insurance and finance is a long-debated and sometimes controversial one. You can find treatises and entire books on the subject. Keep it simple: insurance is insurance, and investments are investments, and it is rare that they should be together in the same place.

CHAPTER 29

PREMIUM FINANCING

"Rich people don't pay full premium for their life insurance; they put up their assets and finance it." This has been a saying for insurance producers, accountants, and financial advisors who cater to a high-net-worth clientele. For many years, this technique of premium financing was a boom to the insurance agents and lenders and a big problem for the insurance companies. It remains a viable method to save money through financing and leverage, but the loopholes have been mostly been closed.

Here's how it works. Say you have an estate of $20 million and your inheritance taxes would be roughly $5 million, prior to 2018 tax reform measures. A seventy-year-old might have an annual premium of $100,000 for a $5 million policy. Instead of the policyholder paying the annual premium, a bank or financial institution would loan the premium and charge interest and fees. If the insured were to pass away before the loan was repaid, the death benefit would go to the lender to pay off the loan, and the balance, would be paid to the other named beneficiaries.

Normally, insurance companies collect premiums for life insurance for many years. Most policies lapse before the death benefit is paid. Why? As the insured gets older, the life insurance costs go up. Many policyholders simply cannot afford these significantly higher premiums, or they choose to drop the policy for other reasons. So, the insurance companies collect the premiums over many years, and statistics show that roughly 70 percent of the time they never have to pay the death benefit.

This is not to say that the insurance companies are bad or take advantage of people. It's simply a matter of economics and actuarial predictability. They are the "house" in Las Vegas. They know the probabilities. The companies must pay death benefits to those few who die before their life expectancy. The peace of mind provided for policyholders in the event of an early death is the reason insurance companies have been in business for more than two centuries.

When a third party becomes involved in the policy, like a private lender or a division of Warren Buffett's Berkshire Hathaway devoted to premium financing, these policies stay in force. The investor-lender will not usually let the policy lapse. If they do, then their interest, fees, and return on investment will suffer or go away completely. So, the policy stays in force, death benefits are eventually paid out, and the insurance company doesn't make as much money if the policy had been dropped and no death benefits had been paid.

Many people acquired these policies as we moved into the twenty-first century. It was certainly a profitable trend for agents, advisors, lenders, and clients. Unfortunately, abuses began to occur. Unscrupulous insurance agents would find an older client, fudge the net worth figures, get the policy issued, and then two years later (after the incontestability period had expired) sell the policy to a third party. The client and agent would usually walk away with a nice profit.

Once the insurance companies caught on to this premium financing trend, applications for insurance were perused more carefully. Questions were inserted into the application about anyone offering to finance the policy or pay the client a fee. Many applications were turned down and agents let go for promoting this technique. In addition, life expectancy tables used for issuing policies were changed. A person was estimated to live a longer life in the revised mortality tables, and therefore more years of premium payments would likely be needed to sustain a policy. The result was that the lenders and financial third parties would theoretically have to wait longer for the death benefits to be paid, thus lowering profits and their return on investment.

Within a few years, the insurance companies managed to close most of the loopholes for this technique, and only truly qualified clients were able to finance their insurance policies using a third party. The tax laws also changed during this time. The inheritance taxes for a married couple with a proper trust would only begin for estates exceeding approximately $11 million. Therefore, fewer clients would need insurance to cover the costs of estate taxes.

Today, premium financing is alive and well, but only for the high-net-worth individuals who can legitimately qualify for this creative technique.

CHAPTER 30

ANNUITIES 101

Some investors feel that annuities are tricky and filled with high expenses and huge exit fees. Others praise the long-term benefits and guarantees of annuities. Andrew Carnegie started an annuity company one hundred years ago that has survived market crashes, recessions, and the Great Depression. The company he founded with $10 million to provide teachers with retirement income and insurance, TIAA-CREF, today is worth nearly $900 billion and has millions of satisfied customers.

Having been on both sides of annuities over the years, I can see why they get a bad rap. Typically, if you try to cash out within ten years, you can be charged surrender fees of 5 to 15 percent in the early going. Annuity salespeople and brokers have been known to conveniently forget to emphasize these severe penalties for withdrawals. Sometimes annuity holders may not remember the consequences of cashing in early. The laws have changed significantly over the years to protect consumers and to make it clear that these are long-term products with severe penalties for early withdrawals.

Let's keep it simple. An annuity is basically a device to guarantee an income for life. It could be the life of the annuitant or the life of a beneficiary, or both. Since annuities are backed by insurance companies that are regulated in their investments to a large degree by the government, there is a perception of safety.

The circumstances that play into purchasing an annuity are the desire for a guaranteed income, tax-deferred growth, and a feeling of security. In some cases, an annuity serves the objective of keeping the principal from being eroded by an heir.

Our firm uses annuities primarily in response to these two statements: "I want a safe place like a CD to save money and use it for income later" and "My beneficiary will spend his [or her] inheritance as soon as he [or she] gets it. I want to provide an income for him [or her] but not access to the principal."

There are many variations of the annuity from the investment side: fixed, variable, or indexed. The fixed annuity provides a fixed interest rate, the variable annuity uses mutual funds for growth and income, and the indexed annuity is tied to a securities index like the S&P 500. Usually there are caps and provisions to limit your potential for growth; however, these annuities usually guarantee your principal and protect against the severities of market downturns.

Here is a common method of solving an estate planning problem by using an annuity. "I don't want my son to receive all the assets and cash when I die because he just can't manage money," says the client. Rather than pay out in a lump sum, the inheritance is divided into cash distributions over many years. In addition, the purchase of an annuity is made to guarantee an income for the life of the heir.

REAL ESTATE

CHAPTER 31

BUYING A HOME

One of the most important financial and life decisions is buying a home. There are so many variables that come into play when purchasing a residence: location, size, number of rooms, yard, neighbors, price, schools, view, privacy, peacefulness, amenities, appliances, surfaces, room flow, distance from work, parks, local services and professionals, nearby medical facilities, etc.

The first order of priority should be to ask: What are the most important things to me in my home? Then, and always at the top of the list for resale and investment value, the selection should be based upon the time-tested mantra: "location, location, location". The most proven adage for purchasing real estate that has the best chance to increase in value is to buy the least expensive property in the most expensive location. This is not always possible or practical, but it is a very good place to start.

After prioritizing your needs and preferences, you can establish a price range. Asking your bank, mortgage broker, realtor, or financial advisor about how much you can comfortably afford is recommended. You can obtain a loan prequalification to zero in on your price point. Usually, it is best to survey several types of possible loans: thirty-year fixed, fifteen-year fixed, interest-only, and adjustable rate mortgages. This procedure should be simple and involves submitting your personal income information, a list of assets and liabilities, and a tax return or two.

With these tools in hand, you can begin your search and the viewing process. My advice has always been to visit at least fifty properties before you make an offer. With the internet, it is easy to sift through the details of properties within your parameters, but there is nothing that takes the place of a personal walk-through of your potential new home. Visiting fifty homes may seem like a big number and a daunting task, but if you've done this homework, you will probably know, without much question, when you have found the right home for purchase.

In addition to the personal viewings, I suggest that you ask for twenty to thirty minutes alone in the home that seems right for you before you make an offer. The realtor or homeowner should be able to arrange this for you. This method will force out the commentary and distractions of other people who may be with you. Listen for your internal voice, walk around as much as you like, hear the sounds around you, imagine yourself living in the home, and pay attention to any adverse intuition or negativity. Unless you are in a big hurry to complete a major purchase like this, you will want take time to *feel* that this is truly the right place for you.

There are other activities that will contribute to making a good selection for your home: walk the street or the building and try to speak with your future neighbors. Visit the schools, the markets, the local parks, and other important places—as well as important people—nearby. You may be in your home for many years, so do your homework.

When you are ready to make your offer, and if it is accepted, try to anticipate if you can live with it financially. Most people will need to stretch their budget to buy the home that fits them best. Usually, this can be accomplished by doing a revised budget and assuming some additional costs. How much will be needed for immediate improvements? What are the property taxes, insurance, utilities, gardening, and other fees and expenses? As part of your offer, a home inspection should be ordered to see what may be "below the surface" of the home: faulty plumbing, roofing problems, termites, electrical issues, air-conditioning and heating systems, etc.

Your first offer should likely be something lower than the listed price. This is normally expected from the seller. Try to ignore many of the pressure tactics from interested parties like "This home will go fast" or "This property will sell for more than the asking price." It's going to be your home, and it's your money. You should always remember that the real value of anything is what someone is willing to pay, not the asking price.

A good realtor will lay out all the possibilities, consider your needs first, and give you valuable advice about making your first offer. There should be no need to worry about or even consider "insulting" the seller with a low offer. It's your life and your money, and a seller will likely listen to any reasonable offer if he or she is truly interested in acquiring a buyer for the home. You don't owe the seller anything in the offer process, and you should not go into any negotiation feeling like this must happen or that you are "married" to the deal.

There may be some back-and-forth price offers, contingencies, or credits. I suggest that you not insist on the seller making any improvements but only to fix the necessary parts of the home. Oftentimes, a buyer asks for a seller to put in a new floor, replace an appliance, or add a fixture. Then upon move-in, the buyer winds up tearing it out or replacing it with something more to his or her liking. For these kinds of changes or additions, I recommend a dollar credit so that you can have what you like and not have to settle for the seller's choice.

Once you agree on a purchase price, then you can select an escrow period and a move-in date. Sometimes a seller can't move out of the home for a while, so you can arrange a lease-back period if necessary. These dates are important and need to be secured with consequences and penalties for not moving out of the property within the time frame. The home inspection should be performed and agreed upon prior to any completion of the purchase.

You should also pay close attention to the deposit parameters. People can change their minds on both sides of the transaction, and there are various ways to avoid a cancellation. Be careful to determine the financial consequences and legitimate reasons for backing out. It may cost you a considerable amount to change your mind. On the other side, the seller should be strongly penalized for not living up to their end of the contract or trying to cancel the purchase without legitimate cause.

When selecting the best loan, go over your budget again, try to predict how long you may stay in the home, and survey your advisors for their opinions. Look for any unusually high fees, prepayment penalties, or possible payment increases in the loan documents. Sometimes banks and financial institutions will try to insist that you leave money with them or open accounts. Unless it is absolutely a requirement, you should not be forced into having more of your assets with the lender.

At the close of escrow, when the home is officially yours, go celebrate. As Dorothy in *The Wizard of Oz* exclaims, "There is no place like home."

CHAPTER 32

HOME MORTGAGES

To paraphrase Forrest Gump: mortgages are like a box of chocolates; you never know what you're going to get. In the past, a home buyer purchased a thirty-year fixed loan with a guaranteed rate, and that was it. You paid the same amount for thirty years and had a deed-burning party when your home belonged to you and not to the bank anymore. Today, you can choose from a wide variety of loan options: fixed rate, variable rate, adjustable rate, VA, FHA, interest only, etc. It can be a daunting decision and very confusing to the average person trying to figure out the best financing.

Begin your search by asking a few questions: What monthly payment can you afford? How much can you put down and still leave enough money for living expenses, retirement contributions, and unforeseen emergencies? How long do you intend to live in this home? (You may change jobs, outgrow the size of the home, or want to change neighborhoods. Try to anticipate the length of time you will be there.) Are you purchasing the home in the hope of short-term appreciation in value? See if you can determine the growth rate of homes in the same area. All the answers to these questions will tie into the type of loan you might choose.

For instance, if you determine that "this is the one; I want to stay in this house forever," then pick a fifteen or thirty-year fixed mortgage, if it is affordable, and call it a day. You'll have the same payment for the life of the loan, and someday you will have your "forever home" paid off, free and clear.

On the other hand, if you intend to be there for, say, five years, and if the interest rates are low, then you might consider an adjustable loan or an interest-only loan for a stated period that fits your anticipated time frame. You may find a loan that offers you level or slightly increasing payments and then converts to a traditional fixed rate, perhaps about the time you are ready to move on to your next home.

If you have served in the military or you are the spouse of a veteran, then you may have government-sponsored loan programs available via the VA (Department of Veterans Affairs). These loans usually include very excellent terms, good rates, and lower down payment requirements. The VA can currently loan up to 103 percent of a home purchase price so that no down payment would be necessary for a home purchase.

Some people qualify for an FHA (Federal Housing Administration) loan. These loans are usually more lenient in qualifications, such as requiring lower down payments and being available to lenders with marginal credit scores. The federal government insures loans for FHA-approved lenders so that the risk of loss is reduced in the event of default.

For most home purchases, especially when rates are low, I recommend that you consider an interest-only loan. Your payment should be the lowest of all the loan types, and you will be in control of paying down any principal at your discretion and comfort level. If you settle into the loan payments and later you want to lower your loan principal amount, you simply send in money to pay down the principal and it reduces the amount you owe. In most amortized mortgages over long periods, the early years have very little principal reduction. Most of the payment goes to interest. By choosing an interest-only loan and paying principal along the way, you are in control of your cash flow and the mortgage balance.

Pick the best piece of chocolate from the box and make a sweet decision about your loan.

CHAPTER 33

PAYING OFF THE MORTGAGE

"Should I pay off the mortgage on my home?" This question has been posed to me frequently as a financial advisor. Before I answer, there is one question that I lob back: "How important is it emotionally for you to own your home free and clear?"

This matter must be cleared up first and foremost. If the answer is along the lines of "I despise any debt" or "My family lost their home to foreclosure," then there is not much else to consider. A strong undertow of personal feelings overcome the financial aspects every time. There is really no need to fight it. The "free and clear" feeling is a very powerful one.

This is the same kind of query that revolves around a long-term-care insurance decision. If your personal experience has been to ride along and suffer with a loved one or friend who lost everything to the costs of a nursing home and health care, then the emotion will simply override the monetary expense.

If the response to the question of paying off the mortgage is similar to "Well, it would be nice not to owe the bank anymore" or "There's not much of a tax deduction left," then a practical financial analysis and discussion can follow.

The first orders of business are to determine the amount left on the loan, the interest rate being paid, the potential appreciation of the home, and the rate of return on investments you hold elsewhere. Let's say the interest rate is 4 percent on the loan, the assumed growth is 5 percent (after expenses), and the investment return on equities or other real estate over time has been 10 percent. Simply put, assuming the same consistency of returns, why would someone choose to add money to a 5 percent growth asset instead of adding to or keeping assets growing at 10 percent?

The second consideration is liquidity. Once the mortgage is paid in full, cash may not be easily extracted. If you need cash, you may have to apply for a home equity line of credit—and now you're back to square one, paying interest again plus loan fees on top. Homes require maintenance and repair. Cash may not be "king" the way it used to be… but having some around for big expenses is almost always a good thing.

Another aspect of a mortgage payoff decision is the risk factor. All investments have their own color of risk: losing value, losing buying power, yielding subpar returns, etc. You should try to measure the risk level of your home's value against the risk level of your other investments. There are a great many ways to measure risk, and there is no such thing as a foolproof technique. If you can obtain comparable prices for homes in your neighborhood and determine appreciation potential based on previous time periods, then you have a beginning point. You can certainly find out the approximate price per square foot on sales of homes with similar amenities.

You should be able to find historical growth rates too. For equities, you can have a risk analysis prepared that uses factors such as price-to-earnings ratios, volatility, standard deviation, and charts. Rental real estate has risk evaluation tools that include cap rates and vacancy percentages.

In the end, it will still be a matter of what is the best emotional and financial decision for you. This is art, not science, and there is no formula for an absolute correct choice about paying off your mortgage. Save yourself some time on this question by asking yourself, "Will paying off my home change my life and give me a strong feeling of security?" If the answer is yes, and you can afford it, then do it. If the answer is no, then analyze the financial aspects before making your final decision.

CHAPTER 34

RENTAL REAL ESTATE

Jerry Buss might be considered the poster guy for building a fortune with real estate. The former owner of the Los Angeles Lakers and the Los Angeles Kings, he was a chemistry teacher at USC who wanted passive investment income from real estate. His first purchase was in the 1960s when he invested $1,000 in an apartment building in West Los Angeles. He found a partner and started a real estate company that continued buying rental real estate. In 1979, he purchased the Lakers, the Kings, the Forum where the two teams played, and a ranch from Jack Kent Cooke, all for $67 million.

Rental real estate carries the same three rules of success for owning a home, land, commercial or industrial property: location, location, location.

There are excellent tax benefits that are available with rental real estate: deductions for expenses, interest, and depreciation. There is also the possibility of a 1031 tax-free exchange of "like for like" properties that can protect you from paying capital gains taxes on profits from the sale of your property. You can trade or exchange an apartment building tax-free with another apartment building as used for investment, but you cannot qualify for the tax-free exchange if you trade your personal vacation home for a commercial building.

These tax benefits come with rules and restrictions, so you'll need a qualified accountant and tax attorney to give you good advice.

Are you ready to be a landlord or landlady—or to pay someone else to do it? This is the essential part of owning personal rental real estate. You'll need to find the property, purchase it, and keep it up. You'll need to locate the tenants and create the lease. You'll need to collect the rent, fix the plumbing, treat for termites, paint, maintain the landscape, pay the property taxes, and deal with tenant complaints. You can hire a management company for about 10 percent of your income to do these things for you.

You can also purchase rental real estate in publicly traded securities through the stock exchanges. A real estate investment trust (REIT) may own thousands of apartments in one fund. You can also find medical, commercial, or industrial real estate this way. These properties can be bought and sold easily. They carry a published price, and they give you great liquidity if you want to take your money out. These publicly traded REITs pay dividends just like collecting your own rent.

With privately owned real estate, your liquidity is significantly reduced. In most cases, to cash out, you will have to go through the real estate sales process and find a buyer.

Rental real estate is a great way to create passive investment income, take advantage of preferential tax treatment, and gain profits with potential appreciation. Privately held investment properties also come with responsibility, so be sure to know what role you are willing to play in the process.

CHAPTER 35

PAPAA BAY

This is a very personal story about enjoying investments during your life. Many people invest money just to make money. Their only enjoyment is in the numbers and the return on their investment. I believe you should also ask, "What do I want my money to do?" For me, there should be a healthy balance of stocks and real estate. Many times, when the equity markets are up, real estate is down. And the reverse happens oftentimes too.

My family spent many summers in Hawaii. We loved everything about these treasured islands: the tropical breezes, the relaxed lifestyle, the sun, and all the joys of being in the ocean. I loved building castles in the sand with my kids and playing in the surf with them or being alone on a surfboard riding the waves. Nearly every vacation, my wife Karen would want to spend some time looking at real estate, dreaming of having a second home in paradise. Finally, we decided to purchase a property there. Our investments in the stock market were doing exceptionally well, and equities were becoming a much too dominant part of our overall portfolio. I said, "We will definitely buy some real estate the next time we go to Hawaii."

We looked all over the island of Maui. We saw homes, condos, and raw land. It was expensive for us, and the island was experiencing the discomforts of growth with relatively crowded beaches in some areas and plenty of traffic. We couldn't find what we wanted on Maui, so we moved our search to the island of Kauai.

Our realtor in Kauai took us from north to south and from east to west. We traversed the island viewing many properties: new homes, fixer-uppers, townhouses, condos, and land. At the very end of an exhausting day, we drove out to an isolated vacant lot overlooking a gorgeous bay. There was nothing but the Pacific Ocean in front of us.

"How far is it to the sand?" I asked.

"About one hundred yards down the path. Let me show you," our realtor said. It was drizzling, and it had been a long day, so Karen decided to stay in the car. The realtor and I walked down the easy slope and arrived at the shoreline. The moment I set eyes on this bay from ground level, the lightning bolt hit me. This was the most exquisite and peaceful bay I had ever seen in my life.

When we got back to the car, I asked about the price and if anyone could build anything between this lot and the ocean. After telling me the price, he said, "No, it is protected by the coastal authority. There will be no structures between you and the ocean." So, I said, "We'll take it." Karen said, "What? Hold on. We are not buying this property today. This is a joint decision. We don't know where we are or anything about this area."

I gave the realtor a check for the deposit and told him that if anyone showed an interest in the lot, he should cash the check and go through with the sale for us. In the meantime, Karen and I would talk about it some more when we returned home to California.

The very next Sunday after our return to the mainland, there was a blurb in the *Los Angeles Times*' Hot Property section that read: "Major film studio owner Peter Guber has purchased an additional fifty acres at Papaa Bay on the island of Kauai." After reading this, Karen asked me, "Where is this property in relation to the lot we put a deposit on?" I said, "It's overlooking Papaa Bay…so Mr. Guber would be our next-door neighbor." Karen said, "Okay. If it's good enough for him, it should be good for us. Let's go ahead and buy it."

Serendipity had made its appearance for us and we proceeded with the purchase.

After several years of thinking about it, we decided to build a home there. The internet had come along, and I was able to manage accounts from anywhere in the world with an internet connection and a phone. It was a fantastic construction project that we enjoyed immensely: imagining, designing, planning, building, rolling with the changes, watching our dream home come true before our eyes.

The timing was right; the stars aligned for us. With this being a financial decision, it was important to have that good balance of real estate and equities—and our purchase has certainly increased in value over the years.

We have spent thirty years loving the life on Kauai. It is a beautiful gem, relatively undiscovered, and still filled with exquisite beaches and places to enjoy the great outdoors. Hopefully, this personal story will not send too many more residents and tourists to the Garden Isle.

We have something that we ask of our friends and visitors: "If you love Kauai, please tell your friends to go to Maui."

COLLEGE

CHAPTER 36

CHOOSING A COLLEGE

Many books have been written about choosing and funding a college education. Breaking down the basics of this topic into one simple chapter is a challenge, but here it goes.

The first thing to determine is if going to college seems even to fit at all. Some people are just not made for school and books and teachers. They should find work related to something they like: a trade, music, art, or perhaps charitable employment. It used to be that a significant percentage of public company CEOs never finished college—their determination, talents, and "street smarts" boosted them to the top. Not so many anymore with the advent of Ivy League college bean counters vetted by boards of directors.

If you are going to lay out a sizable amount of money for a university education, try your best to make sure it's going to be a positive and potentially rewarding experience for you and/or your child. Otherwise, there are plenty of happy, well-earning, and needed carpenters and plumbers in the world today.

Don't get me wrong, I believe very strongly in the values of higher education. "An investment in knowledge pays the best interest," Ben Franklin said. So, if getting a higher education is a powerful motivational value for the family, or if you have a smart, focused child or student, get your checkbook ready. You'll likely need it far in advance of orientation day.

If your child or student shows an interest, shares your high value system, has a good brain, or is meant for a college education, then you will know it early on. It will begin with advanced courses for college credits in high school—maybe even earlier these days. A college planning counselor is usually a good idea. A good counselor is someone who knows the ropes of how to score high on the entrance exams, formulate and make an applicant stand out on complicated and competitive college applications, and help you find financial resources, if needed, to help pay for school. One of the highest annual cost increases of any product or service is college tuition.

Road trips are essential in this process. Arrange the travel to colleges in such a way that you and your child or student will get the widest view. Walk around, talk to students and professors, and get a feel for the vibe on campus. Let your child lead a bit; listen to and watch his or her comments and reactions carefully. There is no substitute for touching and feeling the fabric of the institution. You will want to eliminate schools right away that are academically out of reach or geographically undesirable.

The days when one is accepted into desired colleges are red-letter days and life-changing moments. Opening that envelope, or viewing the acceptance or rejection online, can be like reaching the top of Mount Everest or sinking to the depths of the Atlantic Ocean. There can be a lot of pressure to get in and to receive that cherished acceptance letter. The disappointment of being rejected can also be a terrible pill to swallow.

It is imperative that you set realistic expectations and take your student or child's emotional temperature often during these times. If a major university receives fifty thousand applications and only accepts five thousand applicants, then it seems obvious that these odds of entry should be fully divulged and realized by your student well in advance of decision day.

If your child or student does not get in to the desired four-year college(s) of his or her choice initially, know that there are other roads that can lead to major college entrance. Most four year colleges and universities have "feeder" programs from nearby community or junior colleges. If the student passes the proper courses and maintains a good grade point average at the junior college, he or she is guaranteed entry to the university or college that is part of the feeder program. In most cases, your child or student will enjoy an excellent education from fine professors and not have the intense freshman pressure of a high-level college or university. Many kids who excel in high school and are at the top of the class are discouraged when they experience the competition and the workload that comes with that first year at a major college.

In addition, the financial savings are significant when attending two years at a junior college followed by the remaining years at university. One's bachelor's degree does not indicate the first two years of matriculation. Only the university or college that issues the degree will be displayed on the diploma.

It is my suggestion that for the first two years of study your student should live on or near campus and take a wide variety of courses. The closeness of campus society and social life, coupled with many different study subjects, offers the best introduction to college life. It allows the new student to make friends and to begin focusing on his or her most desirable paths in life.

I am proud to say that my children are all college graduates. My daughter moved to upstate New York, sloshed her way through the snow to work before returning to California. She earned her degree and teaching credential from UC Santa Cruz. My oldest son earned his degree from San Jose State University. He worked in a restaurant at night and drove over the mountains on Highway 17 to attend classes during the day. My youngest son worked in the summers and graduated from UC Santa Barbara and Southwestern Law School. They were imbued with the values of higher education as part of our family culture, and they worked hard to earn their degrees.

Of course, it is part of the great journey in life to find meaningful work. This is one of the hardest things to do. Going to college usually provides a leg up towards meaningful, well-paying employment. College also provides great athletics, personal freedom, intellectual stimulation, and most often some lifelong friends.

Beyond Ben Franklin's "best interest" on your investment, a college education will give your child or student a chance to have fun and grow among other smart young adults. The tuition costs are ominous for most, but the return on investment can be priceless.

CHAPTER 37

PAYING FOR COLLEGE

College and university tuition increase in cost by nearly 4 percent each year, or twice the normal rate of our inflation. So, start saving early and look for free money by way of grants and scholarships. There are many books written and volumes of information out there on this topic. Here are the basics in a few paragraphs:

You may be surprised at how much money is available through the intended school of choice. To acquire these complimentary funds, you will likely need to devote a significant amount of time to doing the research and navigating the application process. The Federal Student Aid system is a good place to begin. If you know the colleges that you want to attend well in advance of their deadlines, then contact the schools directly for their own student aid and scholarship programs.

According to CNN, in 2017 the average cost for private college tuition was just under $35,000. The cost of tuition for a public college for state residents was $10,000. Colleges like Harvard, Stanford, MIT, and Cornell, to name a few, will cost you twice as much. Is it worth it? The college graduate on average earns 67 percent more than the high school graduate.

There are many ways to save and pay for college: through financial aid programs, student loans, and private funding. The use of 529 plans is a common favorite of accountants because these plans provide tax-free growth on your savings for college. There are many rules and restrictions that accompany these 529 plans. You must use the funds for qualified institutions, and there is a maximum limit for contributions. In addition, there are tax penalties for ineligible expenses and specific time frames for withdrawals. The 529 plans are sponsored by individual states, and they have very limited investment choices.

Unless there are compelling reasons to save for college through the 529 plans, I recommend funding your higher education through a simple investment trust. You can establish an independent account on your own and begin purchasing nearly any kind of security that has growth potential. With many years ahead of that first day at college, you can acquire a variety of stocks, bonds, or equity funds that will only be taxed on the dividends that you receive or upon sale of the asset. An S&P 500 Index–oriented exchange traded fund (ETF) would be a good start. There are no limits on how much you can save and invest, there are no restrictive rules to play by—and your investment choices are unlimited. You also have access to the money if you need it sooner for something other than college or university.

No matter when you start saving for college, how you do it, or what your college education costs, your college diploma is more than a piece of paper. The mental hard work and necessary time management of higher education will be testaments to your resolve and persistence. College is one of the most important and satisfying journeys that you or your child will ever take. Hopefully, this education will pay you back with dividends both intellectually and financially. The friends made along the way may last a lifetime.

CHAPTER 38

THE DMV

It's been said that the last place on earth you would want to visit is the Department of Motor Vehicles, a.k.a. the DMV. You can usually expect to be greeted there by crowds, long lines and wait times, lots of red tape, and some rudeness. Even though most of us have been there and must go again from time to time, we will usually steer clear of the DMV at all costs. However, sometimes the government paperwork and bureaucracy have a twist of fate and may turn into a positively memorable experience. Here is my favorite trip to the DMV story.

My youngest son, while going to college in Santa Barbara, bought a car and registered it legally in the state of Hawaii. There was nothing unusual about this since we have a residence there and he thought he might bring the car over some day from California. It was also very cool for him to have a colorful Hawaiian license plate on his car.

When the registration renewal came up the following year, my son and I went to the DMV in Kauai. We arrived about thirty minutes before the doors opened. We were the second people in line. There were two clerks, so we were able to walk right up to the counter. We presented the registration documents, including the required smog certification that was completed in California. The clerk looked over the documents and said, "These are in good order. Is the car parked outside?" No, the car was in California we told the clerk. He said, "Why is it in California and not in Hawaii?" My son and I looked at each other with the same thought: *Uh-oh, what is going to be the best and most correct answer to his question?*

Before we had a chance to think of what to say, something unusually bright and surprising came out of the DMV clerk's mouth. He looked at us with a smile and said, "Would it be that the car is not here in Hawaii because you are going to college in California?"

Amazed at the unexpected helpfulness offered, we both said yes, and the clerk replied, "Okay, then sign here and your registration is complete." We could barely help ourselves from dancing together out of the Kauai Department of Motor Vehicles.

> It isn't necessary to imagine the world ending in fire or
> ice. There are two other possibilities: one is paperwork,
> and the other is nostalgia.
>
> —Frank Zappa

RETIREMENT

CHAPTER 39

FISHING AND COACHING

An investment banker stood at the pier of a small coastal village when a small boat with just one fisherman docked. Inside the small boat were several large yellowfin tuna. The banker complimented the fisherman on the quantity and the quality of his fish and asked how long it had taken to catch them.

The fisherman replied, "Only a little while."

The banker then asked, "Why didn't you stay out longer and catch more fish?"

The fisherman said he had enough to support his family's immediate needs.

The banker then asked, "Then what do you do with the rest of your time?"

The fisherman replied, "I sleep late, play with my children, take siestas with my wife, stroll into the village each evening where I sip wine, and play guitar with my friends. I have a full life."

The banker smiled and said, "I have an MBA from the finest Ivy League college. I could help you. If you spent more time fishing and made more money from selling fish, you could buy a bigger boat. With more fish from the bigger boat, you could use the profits to buy a second boat and ultimately a fleet of fishing boats."

The banker continued, "Instead of selling your catch to a middleman, you would then sell directly to the processor, eventually opening your own cannery. You would control the product, processing, and distribution! You could leave this small village and move to a big city to run your expanding enterprise."

The fisherman asked, "How long will this all take?"

To which the investment banker replied, "Perhaps ten to fifteen years."

"What would happen then?" asked the fisherman.

The banker laughed. "That's the best part. When the time is right, you would announce an IPO and sell your company stock to the public. You would make millions!"

"Okay, then what?" wondered the fisherman.

The investment banker replied, "Then you would retire. You could move to a small coastal fishing village where you would sleep late, play with your children, take siestas with your wife, and stroll into the village each evening, where you could sip wine and play your guitar with your friends."

One of the primary benefits of having money is the freedom to choose what you want in your life. The moral of the fishing story is simple: choosing to have more doesn't necessarily make things any better for you. The fisherman already had a full life. Being content with what you have in your life is one of the keys to happiness—but it really helps to have some money too. There is a surplus of money, you know. It's abundant everywhere. The United States Treasury, for example, loves to print more whenever they feel they might run out. Somewhere in the pages of this book, you should uncover a few ways to create more money for yourself and for your loved ones.

You can have as much or as little as you like, but if your aim is the former, then you simply must find a way to make more. If you don't start out with any money in life, it behooves you to get an education and start on a path to have some money. Thus, the first step is to learn, to obtain an education, and then to create a plan and see it through.

There are generally two ways to get an education: in schools and universities with books, or out on the street, on a job, in the business world. When it comes to business and money, however, street smarts are usually more important than school smarts, at least in my opinion. If you can learn how to survive on the street, tap into what people need and want, then you can make it just about anywhere. It's a different type of education when you go to class and head back to the cafeteria or the dormitory.

Let's stay with the fishing story from the start of this chapter and see what we can learn. You don't suppose the village fisherman took out a book and baited a hook by looking at a picture, do you? He probably didn't learn about a rod and reel from watching a video on the internet either. He most likely learned about hooks, rods, bait, and boats from his father or his big sister or brother. Someone mentored him when he was only tall enough to get a peek over the railing and see the water. This is how most of us learn, by watching and listening to others. So, tip number one, and perhaps the best suggestion in this book, is to learn from exceptional teachers and work with great coaches.

My greatest mentors were my parents, Coach John Wooden, my first sales manager, Dennis Gilbert, and my business partner, Stewart Weissman. Each played a critical role in developing a system and an attitude toward building a successful life. For openers, the desire to succeed must be inside you. The persistence to see things through and not give up—these are also the main building blocks that are crucial for success. You've heard how many times the greats like Abe Lincoln, Thomas Edison and Marie Curie tried and tried before they succeeded. Abe finally became president after losing eight elections. Thomas managed to get a light bulb to flicker on after innumerable attempts. Marie's radioactivity research produced the discovery of two new elements: polonium and radium. Rome wasn't built in a day. Alongside his Pyramid of Success Coach Wooden would write: "Winners never quit. Quitters never win."

The fisherman must have spent many hours learning to thread and tie a hook, find the right bait, tug at the opportune time, and reel in the fish with efficiency.

When it comes to starting a plan for making money and making it last, you begin with a design and a goal. But more important than almost any other element to success is to have the guide, the coach, the mentor to direct you through it. In the National Basketball Association, the players drive, shoot, play defense, and score the points. They are superb athletes with amazing skills. And without Coach Red Auerbach, players like Bill Russell, Bob Cousy, and John Havlicek from the Boston Celtics would not have created a dynasty. They needed Red to mold them, console them, scold them, prepare them, and direct them into a cohesive team of players working hard and playing together. Some people may not remember that Magic Johnson of the Los Angeles Lakers had so much insight and power that he asked Jerry Buss, the team owner, to fire the coach who wasn't "getting it". Pat Riley stepped in as coach, and the championships started coming. Kobe Bryant and Shaquille O'Neal played on the same team for a while and couldn't get to the finals until Coach Phil Jackson came along. And then they won three titles together with Phil at the helm. Shaq and Kobe were driven and hugely talented, but they had been missing the third element of direction and mentoring until Jackson arrived. Phenomenal players need coaches. You will too if you want to succeed at creating wealth and then preserving it.

You wouldn't expect to catch a boatload of fish if you motored out by yourself the first time with a rod and reel and some bait. When it comes to money, the starting point is to figure out how you want to live, what you want to accomplish, and what skills you need to make it happen.

"Catch a fish for someone, you'll eat for day. Teach someone how to fish, they'll eat for a lifetime."

Make your wish list, continue reading these chapters, and find a great coach.

CHAPTER 40

BLOOD PRESSURE

A young couple with two daughters was referred to me. They lived in a modest home in Southern California, and they owned a small construction business. He did tenant improvements on-site for commercial buildings, and she managed the office and paid the bills. We met for financial reviews each quarter for the first year, then semiannually. We went through every conceivable area of money management, including their investments, insurance, retirement, estate planning, real estate, and college education funds. They were working very hard, and they wanted their girls to get a good education—and after that was done, they would try to retire comfortably.

Their business grew. They bought a rental property next door to their home, then another one and a third one. They plowed money into their retirement accounts regularly. Their CPA was a big advocate of socking money away for the future in a variety of tax-deferred vehicles. They had IRAs, SEP IRAs, Roth IRAs, and corporate retirement plans. Their daughters went off to college. Their accounts grew larger, their real estate appreciated in value.

Then one day, her back went out. She developed a serious ailment that was nearly life-threatening to her. Her stress levels went up, and daily medication was needed to control her blood pressure. The husband's sister passed away from cancer at a relatively young age. They had taken care of her during her last days. Their perspective on life changed.

"We can't stand the traffic, the ungrateful and demanding customers, and all the responsibilities anymore. We're stressed out. Our kids are grown up and on their own. Do we have to wait any longer to start a new life, or can we travel and retire now?" Together, we looked at the various sources for income. They were concerned about starting their retirement distributions too early, but I assured them that with their holdings, reasonable expenses, and being relatively frugal, they could do it.

They decided to finish up their existing construction jobs, sell the remains of the business, and move to a more rural, simpler environment. They kept a few rental properties and sold some too. They accessed their business savings and withdrew monthly income from their investment accounts. The tax-deferred retirement accounts were saved for growth and income later.

They packed up their car and drove away from the big city. A few months later, she called me. "We can't tell you how much we appreciate this new life. Thank you for all the money you've made us and the work that we've done together. Our investments have grown so well over the years, and our retirement life and travel are the best thanks to you. We can now enjoy the sacrifices we made. And the discipline of saving for our future is really paying off now. My back is fine, and just last week, I threw away my blood pressure medication."

CHAPTER 41

GETTING OLD

"Getting old is not for sissies."
Bette Davis

An old geezer became very bored in retirement and decided to open a medical clinic. He put a sign up outside that said: "Dr. Geezer's clinic. Get your treatment for $500. If not cured, get back $1,000."

Working nearby, Dr. Young was positive that this old guy didn't know beans about medicine and thought this would be a great opportunity to get $1,000. Dr. Young went to Dr. Geezer's clinic.

Dr. Young said, "Dr. Geezer, I have lost all taste in my mouth. Can you please help me?"

Dr. Geezer said to his nurse, "Nurse, please bring medicine from box 22 and put three drops in Dr. Young's mouth."

After the nurse had done as instructed, Dr. Young said, "Horrible. This tastes like gasoline!"

Dr. Geezer exclaimed, "Congratulations! You've got your taste back. That will be five hundred dollars."

Dr. Young was annoyed. He went back to see Dr. Geezer after a couple of days, figuring he would recover his money. At his appointment, he said to Geezer, "I have lost my memory, I cannot remember anything."

Dr. Geezer said, "Nurse, please bring medicine from box 22 and put three drops in the patient's mouth."

Dr. Young told him, "Oh no you don't. That tastes like gasoline!"

Dr. Geezer replied, "Congratulations! You've got your memory back. That will be five hundred dollars."

Dr. Young left angrily after having paid Dr. Geezer a total of one thousand dollars for two visits. Dr. Young returned in a few days. He said to Dr. Geezer, "My eyesight has become weak—I can hardly see anything!

Dr. Geezer replied, "Well, I don't have any medicine for that, so here's your one thousand dollars back," giving Dr. Young a $10 bill.

Dr. Young exclaimed, "But this is only ten dollars!"

Dr. Geezer said, "Congratulations! You've got your vision back! That will be five hundred dollars."

The moral of this story is that just because you're Young doesn't mean you can outsmart an old Geezer.

The average American male currently has a life expectancy to age seventy-six, while the average life expectancy for an American female is eighty-one years old. When it comes to investing, you simply don't stop trying to make money just because you reach retirement. Although becoming more conservative with your money is natural, there are very few reasons to retire and convert everything to bonds for "safety." Bonds have risk too.

Of course, losing asset value later in life is something to protect against since there isn't as much time to recoup losses. However, a female retiring at sixty-five would have, based on this longevity example, sixteen more years to live and sustain her lifestyle. Therefore, one should continue to invest in a diversified portfolio of investments for the long run, within a comfortable level of risk.

CHAPTER 42

THEY FIRED ME

The essence of this book might just be in this chapter. It is certainly a reminder of the three choices you have about managing money efficiently: make more, spend less, or sell something.

A retired couple came to me after having moved fifty miles south of the rat race and combustion of Los Angeles to the less populated, cleaner, and less frenetically paced Orange County. He had worked on the backstage sets of Hollywood in TV and movies. She was attempting to establish an e-commerce business.

They had a good pension, social security, and a considerable IRA account. We established a game plan and a tentative budget. I began to invest the IRA funds for long-term growth. They owned a large home and had a weekend boat docked in the Dana Point Harbor. They lived a very good life, but not what you might call extravagant. Nevertheless, it was soon apparent that they were spending more than the excellent returns we were achieving in their retirement account. Even with a substantial IRA value, they were taking out more than the minimum required. They were paying taxes on the withdrawals and would soon run out of money at this pace before they ran out of time.

I asked them to come in for a serious heart-to-heart talk. I laid it all out for them. With their projected life expectancies and at their spending levels, they would deplete the funds in their IRA before they reached their seventy fifth birthdays. Then, they would have to rely on their pension and their social security benefits to get them through their senior years. These years could be financially rugged with inflation and the possibilities of assisted living or skilled nursing costs.

There were three choices for us to examine: make more money, spend less money, or sell something. We went over the yields and the returns on their investments. It was hard to imagine making better than the current double-digit returns on their investments without taking significant risks. At their ages, significant risks would be ill-advised. They would not have enough time to make up any big losses.

If they couldn't achieve any higher earnings on their investments without taking extraordinary risks, then how about finding some worthwhile part-time work to supplement their income? We discussed cutting back on their spending. Perhaps they could sell the boat or get a smaller one with lower maintenance costs? Maybe they could downsize their home, save money, and invest some of the sales equity proceeds for more monthly income? I suggested revising their budget and trying to cut down on some of their fixed major costs. "Make more, spend less, or sell something. The choices are yours," I said.

A few months later these clients moved their accounts to another financial advisor. I surmised that our heart-to-heart conversation had not impressed them very much.

The client who referred this couple to me came in about six months later. She said, "Yes, I'm sorry about what happened with you and my friends. They said they fired you because you told them to 'get a job.'" It's funny sometimes to hear how a conversation you had was turned sideways, misinterpreted, or spun around in a way that is, shall we say, incomplete.

A year later, my referring client told me that the couple had parted ways with their boat, left their new advisor, sold their home, and moved to a small farming town in Northern California.

Make more, spend less, or sell something—sooner rather than later.

ESTATE PLANNING

CHAPTER 43

A GIFT IS A GIFT

When people have a lot of money, more than they need to live the lifestyle of their dreams, they begin to give it away. Some give to their families, and some give to charities. Some give to help others or for the tax benefits—or both.

In the distant past, the annual gift tax exclusion was $10,000. A person could give $10,000 to as many people as he or she wished without incurring a gift tax. Currently, the amount of gift tax exclusion is $15,000.

My client was a successful developer who had built homes and golf courses in Los Angeles. He was about seventy years old and retired when I met him. He had come to one of my estate planning seminars with his wife because he wanted to learn about the current strategies to avoid inheritance taxes and to update his own estate plan. He had significant wealth and did not want roughly half of it to be eaten away by estate taxes. He was a true gentleman: kind, considerate, and very generous. When he spoke, his voice and his appearance reminded me of the movie director John Huston.

After several discussions with me, he made an appointment with a tax attorney and revised his estate plan. Using several gifting techniques such as grantor trusts, family partnerships, and insurance trusts, he was able to significantly reduce the tax burden to his heirs. However, that's not the point of this story.

John Huston's look-alike and sound-alike, as wealthy as he was, had no immediate family as beneficiaries of his estate. He and his wife were both in their second marriages, and there were no living children who were directly in line to inherit their fortune. Fortunately, there were many nephews, nieces, and cousins. Counting their spouses and children, there were fifty relatives in all.

At the end of each year, around holiday time, my client would give $10,000 to each one of these family beneficiaries. In addition to these annual gifts, each beneficiary was named in the trust to receive 2 percent of the remainder of his estate after he and his wife passed away. This 2 percent inheritance amounted to approximately $400,000 for each beneficiary.

One year, late in November, I received a call from my client. He wanted to meet with me and the tax attorney. "I want to change my will and trust to eliminate a beneficiary," he said. At our meeting he told us that one of the beneficiaries had come to him and asked for "an advance" of the $10,000 annual gift. This was very upsetting to my client. "This is a gift," he said. "It is not a salary or a bonus. It should not be expected every year, and I do not appreciate the ungratefulness and audacity of this beneficiary to expect or ask for this gift each year. I have given 'the advance' as a onetime courtesy to him, but no future gifts will be given. And I want to remove this beneficiary from our trust!"

My client lived another twelve years. In addition to the approximate total of $120,000 in annual gifts that were not given to this "pushy" beneficiary, he also missed out on nearly $600,000 of the future inheritance because the estate had grown well over the years. This irreverent and presumptive request for an "advance" on a gift ultimately resulted in a cost to this beneficiary of about $720,000.

So, be careful what you ask for. And remember, a gift is a gift.

CHAPTER 44

INVOLVING HEIRS

Keeping secrets means you must remember not to tell. Sometimes this is difficult, and sometimes there's nothing to it. When it comes to telling your heirs about their inheritance, it can be a slippery slope. Many people feel like they can trust their beneficiaries implicitly and they are comfortable laying out all the planning in advance of their leaving this world. Others prefer to keep everything a secret, close to the vest, to avoid conflict. Unfortunately, there is no foolproof or one correct method.

I once received a call from a client who told me that her mother had just passed away. With her father already gone, the estate was going to be split fifty-fifty between her and her brother. She told me that she was meeting her brother after dinner that night to go through her mother's personal possessions and divide them up. When she arrived at her mother's home just after dinner, all the art, silverware, and jewelry and anything else of real value in the house was gone. Her brother had been there earlier in the day and cleaned it out for himself and his wife.

Families have been torn apart by similar acts of selfishness. Oftentimes it is not the brother-sister relationship like the one above that causes the rift; it is a spouse who interferes in the family dynamic. This is the reason financial and estate planning is so important and to put your ducks in a row with proper documentation. It is also a good reason why people with more assets tend to reveal less about their possessions. The will and trust must be created and reviewed regularly to pave a smooth inheritance road.

Here are a few tips on splitting up assets after death: Establishing a proper will and trust certainly must be the starting point. When it comes to distributing personal property after death, the idea of a "lottery/auction" has worked well for many families. Each beneficiary chooses something on their "turn" until all the property has been allocated.

Asset distribution can be specifically described by way of a letter or a schedule in your will or trust. "I want the Picasso to go to my son and my wedding ring to go to my niece." This letter of instruction can be attached to the estate documents, or it can be included within the will or trust. Your attorney and/or advisor should have copies of all updated documents. If desired, an explanation can be made to try to avoid arguments: "My wedding ring goes to my niece because she was always sincere and kind to me. She made me food when I was sick, she drove me to my appointments, and she came to visit me often."

The asset owner can go through the possessions and take pictures of his or her assets. These can be catalogued and recorded so it is known who should inherit each item. One technique that has worked for some people is to physically tag the personal property. For instance, the back of each painting or piece of art could have the name of the intended beneficiary.

Of course, it is best and easiest when beneficiaries are reasonable and flexible. As an example, if children are splitting up personal effects, the first question might be "Who wants what from Dad's things. Is there anything that has special meaning here to anyone?" Should more than one beneficiary make claim to a "special" item, then more discussion can ensue. Sometimes a simple coin toss can settle the claim if no end is in sight.

If the economic values are lopsided, and if it is important to stay relatively equal, then there should be a value placed on each possession. This way, the financial considerations are present and accounted for along with the personal attachment that a beneficiary might have for a meaningful item of personal property. This type of distribution can also apply to real estate or other kinds of property.

Leaving your inheritance in an organized fashion can be simple or complicated. It's up to you and your advisors to create the plan, implement it, and keep the heirs from falling off a cliff.

CHAPTER 45

LOSING YOUR SPOUSE

Two of the toughest things in life to find are great work and a wonderful mate.

Most people have several jobs during their lifetimes. According to the Bureau of Labor Statistics, the average person will try ten different jobs before reaching the age of forty. We know that around 50 percent of marriages in the United States end in divorce. First marriages, a.k.a. "practice" marriages, have spawned long-lasting second marriages filled with love and respect.

When a loving and devoted husband or wife dies, the surviving spouse is usually left with overwhelming grief and a very large void in his or her life. I've certainly attended many client memorial services with tears in my eyes for both the departed and for the survivor.

Invariably, money enters the picture in several ways. Some widows and widowers worry about being able to manage it on their own or outliving their remaining funds. Others want to tackle insurance claims and estate and tax issues, settle things right away. My suggestion is simple: grieve first, and when you're ready, then we can talk about money matters and finances.

A person needs time to process the loss of a spouse. A person in this time is usually emotional and very vulnerable. I ask clients in this situation for a two-word promise about financial decisions for three to six months: "Do nothing!" There should be plenty of time to make important choices, file papers, and figure out your financial life in the future. I say, "We should have a meeting sooner and do some planning but make no major financial decisions for a while please."

Many surviving spouses are ready and able to change their lives completely. They want to begin cleaning out the closets and the garage, putting the home up for sale, and moving on. Maybe they've thought this through in advance and they want to move closer to their children or grandchildren or live in a different environment.

Others are stuck, almost paralyzed, unable to see and accept the reality of a life without their spouse. They have not made any plans, nor do they want to make any plans, for themselves. These are the survivors who really need an arm around their shoulder from a patient listener who cares about their future. It might be a family member, a friend, or someone like me. Surely, I have been in many long meetings, listening, comforting, and guiding with the box of Kleenex nearby.

Following the funeral arrangements and the service, I suggest that the survivor take as much time as needed to be with family. In addition, I recommend that the person begin to make a wish list of anything that comes to mind. It might seem trivial or unattainable, but whatever comes into your head that you think you want, write it down. This will become our table of contents for the book of your future life.

Most clients I've worked with who have lost a spouse get up and go on to manage their personal and financial affairs quite successfully. There is no formula for the time it takes to make this happen. Every person grieves in their own way and in their own time.

In addition to offering these general ideas and financial advice after losing a spouse, I send this handwritten poem:

"So, grieve awhile for me if grieve you must, then let your grief be comforted by trust. If you need me, call me, and I will come. Though you can't see or touch me, I'll be near…and if you listen with your heart you'll hear, all my love around you soft and clear. And then, when you must come this way alone, I'll greet you with a smile and say, 'Welcome home.'"

CHAPTER 46

PULL THE PLUG

All the stories in this book are true. Only minor circumstances have been changed to protect the identity of the characters. I don't believe there is even a faint hint of embellishment in these stories, and certainly none is intended. So here is one that may be truly hard to swallow, but I swear it is completely true to the very best of my recollection. Since it is astonishing—and so vivid in my memory—it surely must be true.

I received a frantic call from the mother of my client. She said that her daughter was in the local hospital's intensive care unit following another episode of overuse of drugs and alcohol. "She's gone into a comatose state, and we will need to pull the plug." I was asked to look through her daughter's trust documents and powers of attorney to determine beneficiaries and the agents for making health-care decisions. I suggested that the hospital or doctor should be contacted for the details of a health-care directive or durable power of attorney. As for the beneficiaries and details of the woman's daughter's trust, I could not reveal anything until the successor trustee of our client's trust was determined.

That evening I went to the hospital to say goodbye to my client. I found her room and went in. She had IVs and tubes running in and all around her. It felt like being in a TV episode of *ER* or *Grey's*

Anatomy. It was very quiet in her room, and she was the only one there. I approached her bedside. She opened her eyes and looked at me. In a seemingly drugged state, but clear as a bell, she took my hand and said, "Mitch, I'm so glad to see you. Please come and sit next to me." What? I was stunned.

For the next few minutes she told me that she had just gotten dehydrated and messed up, but she was going to go to rehab and would get herself up and get straight again. I was taken aback and confused, having come to the hospital expecting to say goodbye to a person on life support, and now I was having a conversation with her about getting better.

The nurse came in and asked me to leave. "It's late. She needs her rest. We're going to start her walking around tomorrow and then move her out of ICU and into rehab." I asked the nurse about my client's physical condition and prognosis, but she would not tell me anything, especially since I was not family.

I left a note for my client's mother saying that I had been there to visit. I added that her daughter had been holding my hand and talking clearly to me about getting better. It sure didn't seem to me that "pulling the plug" was an option. The mother never contacted me again. You can probably figure that there may have been an ulterior motive in there somewhere, or a very different set of interpretations and circumstances.

The story really does have a happy ending. My client went to rehab and recovered fully. She currently smiles a lot and loves her position at a fine international hotel.

CHAPTER 47

WHEN HEIRS RECEIVE THEIR MONEY

It's been said often that you should treat your kids fairly, not equally, because they are not equal. This goes to the heart of making a trust, a will, and an estate plan. Once the heirs receive their money, unless you have put in rules, then they are free to do what they please with what's been left to them.

I have many stories to tell about heirs who have blown their inheritance. I also have stories about those who have made excellent decisions.

It is difficult to influence the actions of your beneficiaries once the money is in their possession, but there are ways to do it. For the irresponsible or incapable heirs, you can restrict access to the principal. You can provide income through financial tools such as special trusts or annuities. You can assign others to monitor and manage their funds even if they are adults.

Unless a client has specifically asked me to restrict beneficiary access to cash, I feel the obligation to try to help the heir make good decisions with his or her new assets. At the core of our financial relationship is my intention to preserve the money that has been given, but in the end, it is the heirs' money, and they have the right to spend it, invest it, or lose it in any legitimate way that they choose.

The most common expenditures by beneficiaries after receiving their inheritance are to pay off debts, buy a home, start a business, or keep investing the money for later use or for their own retirement. One young client expressed it very sensibly:

"My grandmother left this money to me with no strings attached. I've always wanted to start my own business, and this gives me the start-up capital that I need. Maybe I'll lose it all, or maybe I'll make a big success. Either way, I really think my grandmother would be proud of me for taking the chance to become a success."

How can you dispute this reasoning?

If you are leaving an inheritance or receiving one, my suggestions are to think it through, speak with a financial advisor, and make a sound plan for the money. This could be a once-in-a-lifetime gift that may have taken a long time, with a lot of hard work in between, to come to fruition. Squandering it or blowing it without serious consideration would be a shame. The final chapter can only be written by the beneficiary, and hopefully their story has a good ending.

CHAPTER 48

PUT YOUR AFFAIRS IN ORDER NOW

There are countless stories of bad things and bad people that appear when a sizable inheritance goes up for grabs. When the musician Prince died without a will, his estimated $300 million estate was supposedly petitioned by eight hundred "beneficiaries" who claimed a piece of his fortune.

Michael Jackson, Billie Holiday, Pablo Picasso, and Howard Hughes all died without a will. The heirs fought, the lawyers earned fees, and the government extracted taxes along the way. Putting your affairs in order, acquiring insurance, and doing some estate planning are important steps to take to prevent the family from being torn apart. You probably know some brothers and sisters who have stopped talking to each other over the settlement of an estate—or children who have been disinherited.

Here is one sad story of greed and the lengths that shameful people will go to line their pockets.

The worst case of estate gluttony I've known took place suddenly and then unraveled over a period of eighteen months. My friend and client owned a medical office building with a couple of partners. They created a buy–sell agreement to pay off the other partners if one of them wanted to sell early or died prematurely. The partners had purchased life insurance to cover the risk. The building appreciated in value, and my client and his partners wanted to increase the buyout amount. They applied for additional life insurance coverage, but one of the partners could not obtain the new amount of insurance at a preferred cost because of his health. He delayed his purchase, hoping for a better premium rate with applications to other companies. My client put his new coverage in force right away. He made his wife the beneficiary of this new coverage until the procrastinating partner picked up his own higher policy amount.

Then one night, my friend fell out of his chair at home with a brain aneurysm and died. He left behind his two young daughters and his wife.

His partners in the building sued my friend's wife almost immediately for the insurance they claimed was meant for them as part of the buy–sell agreement. They sent subpoena-serving people to the door of the grieving widow at the crack of dawn within a week of his death. They hired an unscrupulous lawyer to file mounds of papers and harass my friend's family into an even deeper state of depression. His wife's parents came from halfway around the globe to support her and were tossed out of the deposition room by the despicable plaintiff's attorney. How low will people go?

As fortune and good sense would have it, the attorney for my client's widow was incredibly smart, a bulldog at interrogation and finding the facts. He was vastly experienced in the courtroom. At the end of the trial—yes, this case went to trial—the judge found in the widow's favor.

In summary, the judge said to the greedy ex-partners and to their lawyer: "You have put this woman and her family through a terrible and unnecessary ordeal. You are the ones who should be on trial in my courtroom."

If you don't have a will or trust, or if you haven't updated yours recently, please go do it now.

CHAPTER 49

MEMORIALS

Two partners in a successful health-care business became my clients and good friends. As I remember, their endeavors were mostly in the development and sales of testing kits for diabetes and other diseases. They were highly educated with excellent business acumen. They both lived active lives. They enjoyed good family living, especially taking pride in their children.

One afternoon, they were both out on the beautiful Newport Beach bay in their speedboats, having fun and going fast, of course. One of the boats hit a wake the wrong way, and the partner was catapulted into the sky and landed heavily back in the boat. He died shortly thereafter.

The families were devastated. The business was going to have some major challenges with the loss of one of its leaders. Fortunately, from a financial standpoint, we had put in place a buy–sell agreement, laid out a succession plan, and funded it with life insurance. So, their business was able to continue with adequate funds from the policy proceeds, and the money was there to provide for their heirs too.

Karen and I attended the memorial service. This was one of the saddest and most uncomfortable moments I can remember, not so much because my friend was no longer with us, but because the religious leader eulogizing him knew almost nothing about him. I'm sure that they had never met, because the words that came out were hollow, distant, and empty to me. Anyone who really knew my friend would have been able to describe his great intellect, his sense of humor, his love of family, his friendship, and the way he lived his life to the fullest. This eulogy was not in any way a fair tribute or proper send-off to my friend.

This eulogy disturbed me so much that I went home and immediately wrote some things down on the computer about what I did and did not want for my own funeral. A little macabre, perhaps? To me it wasn't really self-directing a memorial service or writing my own eulogy; it was simply an act that was borne out of frustration, and a message to avoid the pitfalls and disappointment of my friend's memorial service.

In my suggestions, I asked that only people who knew me be able to speak. I wanted the music of the Beatles, the Rolling Stones, Crosby, Stills, and Nash, Bob Dylan, Janis Joplin and Elton John to be played. It was important to acknowledge my friends and family who were by me along life's pathways. I suggested a chorus of "Bali Hai" to be sung by everyone. I wanted it to be said that life can be great by trying to make the world a better place. Stories and memories of the good times should be told, and a party should ensue.

After writing these wishes down in my computer, I felt better about things. I returned from thinking about death and memorial services to living in the present again.

A few days later, Karen took me aside and asked me, in a very serious tone, "Are you not telling me something that I should know? Do you have something bad going on with your health? Are you sick and dying?" I told her none of these things were true and asked her why she would think this way.

She said, "Well, I happened to see your personal funeral wishes that you left up on your computer."

ADVISORS

CHAPTER 50

CHOOSING AN ADVISOR

Whether it's nursing or car repair or financial planning, I believe that you can make a good delineation between people who really care about you and those who are in it primarily for themselves. Of course, most people have some degree of both in them. The purpose of this chapter is to persuade you to try to avoid the ones who are selling something and don't really care about you. I encourage you to try to find the ones who are sincerely being of service and do care about you.

Let's take nursing as just one example. Aren't you pretty much able to tell the grumpy ones from the pleasant ones? There are nurses who are there with a smile and a comforting disposition no matter what time of day. They thrive on making you feel better. They are patient and loving and committed to their service to others, especially those who are in pain. Then there are the nurses who are regularly looking at the time to see how much longer they have until their shift is over. They may be doing their job, but not with the same feeling and inner devotion.

I have been fortunate to have known some loving and devoted nurses in my life, so I'm certainly not picking on this profession. I say these things simply to point out that, in every service business, there are professionals who really care. If they are skilled in their work and they care, then these are the types of professionals you should try to find.

In the wide world of financial services, we have many types of representatives: registered investment advisors, certified financial planners, chartered life underwriters, bankers, mortgage brokers, analysts, insurance reps, retirement consultants. The list is long and varied.

When choosing a financial advisor, the first question to ask is "Do you represent me, or do you represent the company? In other words, who signs your check?" This is one easy way to find out if you are going to come first or take a back seat to the company.

If a representative, consultant, or advisor works for a company, you'll almost always be in second place. Their main job is to make money for the company and for themselves. You can spin it or try to cut it any which way, but in the end, this is the reality. These representatives are typically in the business of sales, not so much service. Sometimes the lines cross, and a company person can really care about you and provide you with excellent service. However, this person will be looking over their shoulder for the company's plan, not necessarily your plan first.

Unfortunately, there are many unscrupulous types of company reps who will attempt to sell you anything, especially if is good for their personal bank account. This is a good reason we have government and industry law enforcement authorities—to try to protect us against selfish and dishonest salespeople.

The financial industry has a great many devious characters. These terrible people have bankrupted investors and even brought world economies to the brink of disaster. Charles Keating, the banker, and Bernard Madoff, the wealth manager, are two of the most devilish financial people ever to have lived.

When Keating's Lincoln Savings failed in 1989, it cost the federal government over $3 billion. Approximately twenty-three thousand customers were left with worthless bonds. In the early 1990s, Keating was convicted in both federal and state courts on many counts of fraud, racketeering, and conspiracy. He was sentenced to 12 years in prison.

In March of 2009, Madoff pleaded guilty to eleven felony charges and admitted to a massive Ponzi scheme that defrauded investors out of approximately $18 billion. He stole from just about everyone: wealthy individuals, companies, sports teams, and even charities. He was sentenced to 150 years in prison.

Movies such as *Wall Street*, *Glengarry Glen Ross*, and *The Wolf of Wall Street* have cinematically depicted this type of corrupt and unprincipled behavior. These are extreme examples of dreadful investment people who cared only about their own personal fortunes at the expense of others.

Let's turn now to trying to find those who really care. The first order of business is to find out if they have products to sell you and to ask questions. Are they self-employed? What is their track record? Can you speak with their clients or advisors? Is the advisor or representative fee-based, and if yes, what are the fees? Are there special products or promotions that might be part of any financial recommendations for you? Will there be any hidden expenses? Who will be the financial institution serving as custodian of your investments? Will these investments be publicly held or privately traded? What is the frequency of investment reports, and from what source are these reports generated? What is the experience and the expertise of the financial professional? Who are the other team members, such as accountants, attorneys, and associates?

Using the internet today is an excellent way of vetting an advisor, although it can be flawed and should not be relied upon entirely. It's easy to create a website and perhaps fool people into believing its legitimacy. In the final analysis, it is always best to speak directly with people who have worked with the person you are considering as someone to help manage your money.

Like a wonderful nurse, you should take note of some simple signs of a caring financial professional. Are they truly listening to you, paying attention to your needs? Do they ask about your family and your "wish list"? Have they designed a plan that speaks to your risk tolerance, your time frame, and your personal considerations? Do you get the feeling of give-and-take and collaboration? Are they looking at the clock or looking at you? Do you feel pressure to sign up right away? Will you receive a written plan or "blueprint" for your investments? Do their ideas incorporate expensive, exclusive, or proprietary products? Do you sense kindness and integrity in their methods and demeanor?

If you can answer yes to most of these questions, you're on the right path to choosing someone who cares about providing real service to you.

CHAPTER 51

TWO SIDES OF MONEY – THE ACTRESS

There are two sides to money, in my view: the practical side and the emotional side. Both are critical to making good financial decisions. For instance, the following question has been voiced by clients very often, and it is at least two-sided: "Should I purchase long-term-care insurance?"

The first side of the answer can be emotional. If someone has experienced a friend or family member depleting assets by spending them on assisted living or skilled nursing, then it is a deeply felt question and outweighs the practical side of the answer. There is rarely a reason to continue exploring the financial need for such a purchase if the person is feeling a strong urge to avoid any possibility of his or her own financial demise as experienced by someone he or she knew.

On the other hand, if it is a decision based upon financial merits and not driven by emotions, then it is important to have the discussion about costs and benefits. Other emotionally charged decisions can be about paying off the mortgage, buying property, sending one's children to a certain college, or even deciding to be married or not. These decisions usually contain an emotional element that must be considered before moving forward.

As a part of our initial meeting with a new potential client, I suggest two things. First, I tell my visitors that no money will exchange hands on our first "date", so there is no reason to bring a credit card or a checkbook. Second, I mention that this meeting will be about getting to know each other—beyond just the financial aspects of what we might do together.

My questions in our first get-together are not only about assets and liabilities, investments, and financial goals. I want to know about the person's past experiences that may have shaped his or her tolerance for risk. Did the client lose money in a bad investment? Whom does he or she feel closest to within his or her circle of family and friends? This inquiry could determine who might be best to serve as trustee for the client's estate.

I want to know what my clients read, what they believe, which pages on the internet they view first, what they consider to be their ideal vacation, and what they want their money to "do" for their family, their community, or society. These touchy-feely questions are very important to establishing a long-term relationship and allowing me to know what people choose to avoid and what makes them feel good. I feel that it is imperative as an advisor to know your client deeply.

I once competed with four other advisors to become the investment manager and advisor for an Oscar-nominated actress. The accountant who was organizing the meeting asked me if I wanted to go first or last. Usually, I would have chosen to be the last act, but I felt that the actress would probably be tired of being pitched to for an hour by the time the last guy came up to bat, so I went first.

The meeting took place in a luxury conference room on a high floor of an office building in Century City. When I entered the room, the actress was seated at the table, comfortably dressed in jeans and a sweater. She was very lovely in a casual way; different from her many leading roles as the beautiful woman on the big screen.

The first question I asked was, "What is your first memory of money?" Without hesitation, she said, "That is such a great question. I can tell you exactly my first memory of money. I was eleven years old. I was in Europe as a child actor, and my dad was with me and acting as my agent at the time. We had an afternoon off from shooting the film, and he gave me twenty dollars for spending money. I bought something for myself, and I came back with ten dollars. I will always remember the look on his face and the way he told me how proud he was of me." She had experienced an emotional connection to money from her childhood interaction with her father.

We spent the next forty-five minutes getting to know each other. We talked about our parents, our children, movies, business, travel, and many areas of finance. It was a warm, smart, and very personal conversation. When I walked into the lobby and saw the other four guys sitting there going through their presentation papers, I knew that choosing to go first had been the right decision. Less than two hours later, the accountant called and told me, "You have a new client."

CHAPTER 52

THE MESSY AND DISLOYAL CLIENT

On the John Wooden Pyramid of Success, the foundation is made up of five blocks: Industriousness, Enthusiasm, Friendship, Cooperation, and in the very middle of the base, Loyalty. In business, and in relationships, there is rarely an attribute more critical to success than loyalty.

Sometimes being loyal and committed is just not warranted. You may really feel obligated to someone or be in his or her corner come hell or high water, but if this person turns out to be incompetent or unscrupulous, you should part ways. On the other hand, when you've done good things for someone who turns out to be disloyal and unappreciative, it is hard to forgive and forget.

I was introduced to a woman who had a multiple of problems going on in her life. I should have sent her on to another advisor right away. She turned out to be my biggest client mess. She had sizable assets and a hefty monthly income, but she was truly in financial and mental disarray. Her ex-husband was threatening to cut her off from her alimony and child support. The IRS was breathing down her neck for back payments and interest. Her financial advisor was also her accountant. He had sold her high-commissioned annuities and put her money into expensive, front-loaded, and inappropriate mutual funds. She was renting a home in a neighborhood she didn't like at all, and her children were hardly speaking to her. She had been referred to me by a good client and she really needed someone to help turn her life around. So, Mr. Phelps, I chose to accept the mission even though it truly looked impossible.

The first items were to deal with the ex-husband and the IRS. I asked our forensic CPA to examine the books, dig into the ex's finances, check on the IRS demands, and come up with a plan. Within two weeks, we had straightened out the IRS notices and relieved her of more than half the duplicate and unnecessary fines and penalties connected to her taxes. From our attorney, a strongly worded message was delivered to the ex-husband to be sure to continue his alimony and child support payments. Duly warned about the consequences, he readily agreed.

She now had three professional advocates standing next to her to help start making things go her way.

Next, she let go of her accountant aka investment advisor aka insurance agent. The trust and retirement plan assets were transferred to our advisory service, and we made the appropriate changes. The accounts began to grow almost immediately as the high-cost mutual funds were eliminated along with the inappropriate fixed-income funds.

We must have met at least half a dozen times with our new client and her new accountant in the first three weeks of our new collaboration. She was perking up, worrying less, and getting her life in order.

Then we moved on to finding her a better home. She had been inundated with solicitations from realtors from her business and her fitness club. I suggested that she find one good realtor to work with who seemed to understand her needs. I advised her not to make any decisions until she had visited at least fifty homes for sale. After experiencing a variety of homes and neighborhoods, she would know the right home when she walked into it. After a few months, she acquired the home of her dreams in a great neighborhood. Of course, it needed some work.

With the assistance of her new advisory team, she interviewed several contractors. She found one who came in with a workable budget that was reviewed and adjusted by her advisors. Ultimately, she was able to remodel her new home to her specifications, although we cut back some of the projects to keep within her budget. After she moved in to her new digs, her visits to our office were accompanied by a big smile on her face instead of the frown and exhausted eyes of a person carrying a big bag of worries.

In addition to helping her with the ex, the IRS, the former accountant, the realtors, and the contractors, we also became a watchdog for her home loan and bank transactions. At the outset, the lender was asking for all her cash and liquid assets to be held in their bank to qualify for a good loan. By the time we'd finished, we had removed the "all or nothing" deposit contingency and found a lower interest rate than the one originally offered. She acquired the home she had dreamed of with a lower monthly cost than the rent she had been paying in a home and neighborhood she didn't even like.

We helped her reorganize her medical practice, having found and established the best entity for tax purposes. We assisted her in arranging instant credit card payments and helped her with the slow-to-pay insurance reimbursements. She found a new office location, and many of her patients followed her without hesitation.

As she met and resolved these fiscal and lifestyle challenges, her relationship with her children began to improve. They sensed and watched as her confidence was being rebuilt. They listened less to their father about her faults and started coming over to be with her for lunch and dinner. Positive karma was being produced at nearly every level of her life.

Unfortunately, it was a short-lived collaboration for us. After all the work, the care, the consultations, the fixing, and the patching, she turned her back on her team and jumped ship. She moved her accounts from us and told the CPA off. *Poof,* we were yesterday's news. The "what have you done for me lately" syndrome had knocked on and broken down her door. I'm not sure why she departed, even though I asked her and attempted to find any mistakes that we might have made along the way.

Her reasons for the backdoor exit were not really that important to me. As the first of the Nine Promises for Happiness says, "I promise to forget the mistakes of the past and move on to greater achievements in the future." So, I just felt disrespected and disappointed for a little while and then moved on to being with the clients who appreciated us.

People who act so disloyal and unappreciative can leave scars and discourage you from putting out your hand and helping again. Nevertheless, it should not stop any of us from continuing to find and to be with people who know the importance of loyalty.

CHAPTER 53

UNAPPRECIATIVE BECOMES APPRECIATIVE

Most of us have people in our lives with a disposition that is generally negative and unappreciative. These whiners and complainers sometimes can change miraculously and start giving compliments and showing their gratitude.

One of our clients had some particularly difficult losses and challenges in her life that defied preparation. She lost a vibrant and devoted husband quite suddenly and at a very early age. Her children were troublesome with drug problems and abusive marriages. Soon after her husband died, she was left with taking a young grandchild into her home and raising him through his teen years. Not an easy task for any parent, let alone a grandparent in mourning.

She constantly bemoaned her lot in life to me during our meetings. She made many detailed requests and required a great deal of explanation and service from us. Oftentimes I thought about asking her to go to another financial advisor.

One day, after several years together, she called me and asked me to change the beneficiaries on her retirement accounts. "I've been to a new lawyer, and he told me that the beneficiary of my IRA should be my living trust. So please remove my children by name and designate my trust as the beneficiary of my retirement plan."

This was not the first time this type of request had been made of me, but it is usually a wrong plan of action. There are few decisions that are black-and-white in the financial and estate planning process. For almost all clients, this one is clear-cut for nearly every circumstance. If you name a person as a beneficiary of your IRA, then that individual has potential tax savings available to him or her when the proceeds are distributed. One very significant benefit is to roll over funds to an inherited IRA and defer the taxes. A trust named as beneficiary does not receive this type of tax savings deferral benefit.

Rather than simply accept the client's instruction, I explained the potentially negative consequences of her action and suggested that she seek another opinion. Grudgingly, she said she would and hung up.

Several weeks later I called her. The first words out of her mouth were "I have to thank you so much for your advice. You were right. I would have made a big mistake by designating my trust as beneficiary of my retirement investments. I checked with my CPA and another attorney, and they both agreed with you. I really appreciate your concern and being persistent about the right information. You were trying to make sure that I did the right thing for my family—and I did."

Appreciation can sometimes arrive from people who have been unappreciative in the past, especially when they realize that you are truly looking out for them. Usually, good things take time when it comes to money—and often in relationships too.

CHAPTER 54

WORK AS CONTRIBUTION

One way to show our appreciation for our clients was to have a beautiful and delicious birthday luncheon at a great restaurant every three months. We would invite the clients who had birthdays in the most recent quarter, asking them each to bring a friend or relative. Gifts and prizes were handed out, and a brief economic update was given.

I enjoyed greeting each birthday client and his or her guest as they entered our private room in the restaurant. At one luncheon, I was taken aside by a guest who asked to speak with me privately. She was the best friend of a lovely client who had recently lost her husband to a sudden heart attack.

People need time to grieve and to put their own lives in perspective after a life-changing occurrence. They are usually overcome with emotion, and the world can be spinning out of control. They are certainly not in a place to make any serious financial decisions. I urge them to take time to grieve and advise them against signing or committing to anything money-related for about six months. If anything at all comes up to discuss, or if they need a shoulder to lean on, a hug, or just to talk about their loss, then they can reach me anytime or anyplace, 24/7. The Kleenex box on my desk has been well used over the years.

Our guest expressed her thanks for the chance to meet me in such a relaxed and lovely atmosphere. Then she started in:

"I have to tell you that my friend could not have made it through her terrible time without you. She told me how the loss of her husband had devastated and paralyzed her. She said that she had called you and met with you often and that you were the only man in her life she could truly trust and who would listen and just be there for her. Saving my friend is really what I want to thank you for most."

Imagine my feelings when hearing these kind words. My job is not simply managing money and financial planning; it is more about contributing to the quality of life for my clients. You would be hard-pressed to find a more poignant description of work that has truly made a positive impact on someone's life. This kind of compelling compliment gives me the reason to get up early every day and do what I do.

Soon after this luncheon, my client's friend opened a substantial account.

CHAPTER 55

TRAGEDY, SECURITY, AND LOYALTY

"You are the longest relationship in my life, except for my own family," she told me. These words came from a client of more than thirty years. She had a tragic story, very similar to one shared by her friend who had introduced us and who had been working with me as a client for several years.

In their thirties, these two special women lost their first husbands, police officers who were killed in the line of duty. Each widow received the same extensive benefit package: an income for life, fully paid insurance, and college funds for their children.

Even with generous survivor benefits from law enforcement, both women continued to work and earn a good living. They knew instinctively, and from speaking with other widows of fallen officers, that they must continue to save and manage their money wisely for a long time. The widows' benefit packages were generous but not large enough for them to enjoy extensive travel and some of the extras in life. Ultimately, they rolled over most of their assets to our advisory firm.

They had lost their partners to tragedies and gained some financial security, if there is such a thing. Although they knew the perils of their husbands' occupations, they were shocked, their worlds were upended when their husbands were killed.

Today, these two amazing women are happy, living full lives, and extremely proud of their successful kids. One son is a police officer working to protect his community, just like his father. Another son is in the military protecting his country, while another child is becoming an attorney to protect those in need. The acorn doesn't fall far from the tree…unless there's a big wind.

With their mothers' watchful eyes and guiding hands, each child earned a college degree, graduated from the police academy, or achieved an advanced military education. These adult children honor both parents as responsible and contributing adults to make our world a better and safer place.

It has been extremely rewarding to work with such outstanding women—graceful and appreciative people who have shown perseverance and loyalty for nearly a lifetime.

CHAPTER 56

HOUSE CALLS AND HEROES

In the early going of client gathering, I made house calls. Driving to someone's home to make it easy on them or to expedite a get-together was enjoyable. Unless they had cats or a lot of dust—and then my allergies would kick in and the meeting would be very brief.

One of my clients always required a house call because she couldn't really leave her home most of the time. It wasn't because she was disabled or had no means of transportation. It was simply that her chosen charitable work had to be done at home. To this day, I have never met anyone who has done a similar thing and had the incredible patience to provide this special gift to others.

This woman's chosen way of contributing to the world was to temporarily accept infants born from drug-dependent or alcoholic mothers and care for them while weaning them from the substances in their systems.

If an alcoholic or drug-dependent mother gave birth to a child, a responsible hospital or physician would not allow the birth mother to infect, abuse, or abandon her newborn. The mother would be sent to rehab, and the child would be sent to my client.

Imagine the pain and suffering these infants experienced. My client would hold them tight while they screamed incessantly during those first few days. She comforted them, gave them vitamins, fed them formula, and loved them constantly until their vulnerable bodies were fortified and stabilized. She was up at all hours of the night and day. Our financial reviews usually required me to follow her around the house while she bottle-fed the child or tried to rock the child to sleep.

Following this amazing care and parental bonding of several weeks, she would then return the newborn to her drug- and alcohol-free birth mother or to social services. What a heroine!

This client and I have known each other now for three decades. Her grown children have become clients. It is a great pleasure to serve such wonderful people who have contributed so much to those who cannot make it on their own.

CHAPTER 57

COLLEAGUES INSIDE AND OUT

Six was the magic number of years for working together with my assistant, my colleague, my main person. Surely it wasn't for lack of pay, consideration, or trust that each of my assistants left after six seasons together. The timing was simply right for them to say goodbye.

My very first administrative assistant was a lovely young woman who was just starting out in life. She was welcoming and attentive, customer service oriented, and smart. She headed to law school after her time with me and became a successful attorney in Philadelphia.

My second colleague in the same role could best be described as extremely family oriented with a caring disposition far above the norm. She writes a single-spaced, two-sided holiday letter each year about all her family happenings. She was soft-spoken but vigilant and determined to keep my appointment book filled with meetings and potential clients. When she left after six years, it was to go back to teaching students with disabilities. "I just want to return to my other work. It would make me feel better to know that I am doing good in the world by helping kids."

Number three assistant was a dynamo, politically energized, and inclined to make the world better by making it green and socially responsible. She was a proud immigrant who related well to people in a deep sense. She taught me a great deal about bamboo and the benefits of appealing to clients who wanted to do things ecologically and ethically. She was one of my first introductions to socially responsible impact investing with green funds and ESG (environmental, social, and governance). She departed to Santa Barbara after our six years together to take care of her ninety-four-year-old ailing father.

Assistant number four was also very sensitive and loving. She was a single mom raising two young children, mostly on her own. The kids were in their formative years, going to elementary school and middle school. She helped me build our business in a very caring manner, all the time with protective eyes and ears open for any issues with her children's school, friends, babysitters, etc. At the six-year point of our working relationship, she met a great guy, got married, gathered up her children, and moved away with them.

Today, my go-to-person, our director of client services, has broken through the six-year cycle. She says, "This is my dream job. Why would I want to go anywhere else?" She has all the attributes of my former colleagues and more. She has a great love for her family, her friends, and our clients. She has tremendous integrity and intelligence, and she truly understands that customers come first. We have grown our business extremely well during her tenure. She deserves many kudos for our 99 percent client retention rate. I always hear her laughing with clients and see her catering to their needs, hugging them, and making them feel special.

It is truly a compliment to be able to stay in touch with these fine women who have helped me along the way. Most of these ladies maintain their personal investment accounts with us. They certainly know how much we care for clients and how much money we've made them. They know how our business works, inside and out, and I am eternally grateful to them.

CHAPTER 58

DANCING FOR GREAT SERVICE

What is it about great service that makes us happy? For openers, I would submit that a feeling of care and personal attention, quick satisfaction of our needs, and getting the job done efficiently are three good answers. Whether it's the refrigerator repair person, the car valet, the accountant, or the doctor's receptionist, being friendly and showing genuine concern, responsiveness, and expertise are important elements of great service.

With nearly one million employees at Walmart back in the day (there are over two million today), founder Sam Walton was known to answer his own phone. If he could do it, really any organized service person can do it. At our office, we try our best to pick up the phone on the first ring with a smile on our faces. My service motto has always been, "If you contact me and I don't get back to you within twenty-four hours, then I'm either dead or didn't get the message."

It shows respect to treat people like they are first in line and that they matter to you. It's hard to imagine being busier than someone like actor Tom Cruise, Britain's Princess Diana, or Cal Ripken during his record of 2,632 straight Major League Baseball games for the Baltimore Orioles. These public figures are known to have spent extraordinary time with children, sick or underprivileged people, and fans from all walks of life. Tom is famous not only for his action films but also for the innumerable photos he takes with fans and the autographs he signs along the red carpet at movie premieres. Diana was known as the "people's princess," tirelessly active in the removal of land mines and fighting the AIDS virus around the globe. Cal could be seen two or three hours after a game still signing balls, bats, hats, and gloves, until every fan there had his autograph.

Sometimes we have many balls in the air to juggle or we feel like a triage nurse trying to find the most severe injuries to treat first. Most of the time, we can prioritize and give our full attention to the person who is there in front of us or on the line. Another mantra we follow is simply "Do it now."

Our firm usually has a big client appreciation event at the end of the year to "hug" our clients. It's held at a beautiful venue with fine food, entertainment, and charitable intentions. There is no pitch or promotion; we simply want to spend some extra time and money to show appreciation to our loyal clients. One year, we had a theme of "Dancing with the Clients." I asked several clients secretly in advance of the dinner event if they would be willing to dance in front of our guests. They would be matched up with one of a few professional dancers we hired. They would go to a back room for twenty minutes, learn and practice a few ballroom dance moves, and then return to perform. I remember asking one client who told me that she was really into hula dancing. "You mean that I would get a chance to dance and embarrass myself in front of hundreds of people at your event? I'm in," she said.

Our three clients performed with nervous joy and enthusiasm. The audience cheered loudest for the winner, and all three participants received their very own "mirror ball trophy" for their dance.

The first-place winner thanked me and said, "I wouldn't be here without the incredible service we get from you. Now, I have also had the most fun of my life."

CHAPTER 59

MEETING EXPECTATIONS

We strive to treat our clients fairly. Some people want nothing to do with money management: "I'll be hiking in the Himalayas, so please do what you do best and just be sure my check is deposited at the bank. Thanks." Other clients are managing their investments every day, watching and listening to the business channels and even making trades in their accounts in addition to consulting with me. We offer our services to people with all levels of client involvement.

A few of our clients request a tailor-made spreadsheet each month with their personal preferences. We accommodate them because they are committed to us and appreciative of our work. One client loves to pick apart our performance and challenge us to do even better. Another client asks with a grin, "So, did we double our money this month?" I regularly field calls and emails about stock tips, investment suggestions, market warnings, and mostly clients needing a bit of reassurance. The ideas, compliments, and criticisms can border on Monday morning quarterbacking but are usually worth the extra time and effort. Like most business and professional people, I find that a challenge from a client can be a great way to improve my performance and try to jump over an even higher performance bar than one I might set for myself.

One day, our very challenging and very detail-oriented client referred us to a friend who lived across the country. We were unable to get together in person, so we talked several times on the phone. As we reviewed his personal financial goals and concerns, he seemed a bit hesitant about the distance and the change of advisors. He needed to feel trust and confidence in starting with a new firm. He wanted to transfer his accounts to our service, but he needed just another ounce of confidence.

Then he asked the one question, and received the answer, that removed his last bit of reluctance: "My friend who referred you can be the most demanding guy. He reads financial reports, watches every dollar and needs a lot of attention. How long has he been working with you?" When I said that his friend, and most of his friend's grown children, had been together with us for a decade, he said, "If he has been with you that long, you must be able to meet his very high expectations. Let's get started and open the account."

CHAPTER 60

THE HOLLYWOOD BOWL

As mentioned previously, I spent many summer evenings as a teenager at the wondrous Hollywood Bowl. I was climbing hills and trees with my brothers and friends to sneak into the Bowl or watch from afar the greatest musical acts of the 1960s: Jimi Hendrix, Janis Joplin, the Jefferson Airplane, the Mamas and the Papas, the Doors, the Rolling Stones. The only top group I missed were the Beatles in 1965. *Darn.* Sometimes, we were fortunate to have a legitimate ticket and even a backstage pass courtesy of a friend who knew the manager of the Doors at the time.

There are moments in a great rock concert that are akin to seeing the red lights of a police car in your rearview mirror. The adrenaline rush is extremely high. Seeing Jimi play electric guitar with his teeth or watching Janis belt out "Piece of My Heart" from twenty-five feet away gave me feelings of exhilaration that have stayed with me for fifty years. In those moments, you can lose control and enter a euphoric state of mind. The world around you just goes away, and you are lost in time with a wall of sound running through and around you. Giving up your past and present, sucked into that moment, you are momentarily out of control and in a highly charged place, and no drugs need to be involved.

How do rock-and-roll experiences tie into managing your money? In a Peter Pan world of never growing up, my youthful days of being in the center of a musical nirvana created in me visions of everlasting adolescence. Most of us realize later that we will grow up and eventually deal with money. There is the alternative of dying young like Jimi, Janis, Jim Morrison, and Amy Winehouse all at age twenty-seven.

Some of us learn about money early in life, and the knowledge stays with us. We budget, we plan, we create goals and dreams, and we try to stay on the right path to reach those goals. Perhaps you remember your first experience with money?

Some of us will turn the finances over to someone else to manage them. If you find the right people to help, this can be a huge advantage in life. There were some outstanding rock-and-roll managers who guided, organized and accumulated great wealth for their musicians: Tom Parker for Elvis Presley, Irving Azoff for the Eagles, and Brian Epstein for the Beatles are the first names to come to mind.

There is also the connection between a great musical experience that grabs our emotions and makes our hearts skip a beat and the "noise" in the media today that wants to excite us in a different way. And today's noise is little different at its core than the noise of fifty years ago.

When the guy on TV today says the market could lose 50 percent, it can scare the living daylights out of you. Imagine losing half of your investments. You can smile at the sensationalizing broadcaster, watch more, or switch it off. It's no different today than what Mick Jagger sang in *Satisfaction*: "When I'm drivin' in my car and that man comes on the radio, he's tellin' me more and more about some useless information supposed to fire my imagination."

If you have a goal and a plan, if you diversify your investments, and if you work with good money people, you will have an excellent shot at achieving financial satisfaction and success.

SUMMARY

Hopefully, you have enjoyed reading these chapters and have been entertained while learning something about money management. As we come to the end of this book, I am reminded of a scene with Robin Williams in the movie *Mrs. Doubtfire.*

He's working a menial backroom job at a TV station. After watching one of the on-screen personalities give a very boring lesson to kids about dinosaurs, Robin's character steps on to the stage set after everyone has gone home. He thinks he's all by himself. He picks up some plastic dinosaurs and begins to use his incredible energy and a variety of voices to breathe life into the T. Rex and the brontosaurus. He's in his own Broadway play, using the impressions of Elvis Presley and James Brown to bring these extinct beasts into the here and now.

Unbeknownst to Robin, the station owner is watching in the wings, listening to and smiling at the thoroughly engaging improvisation. Robin's comedy and versatility is simply incomparable. Of course, the station owner recognizes Robin's entertainment and storytelling talents and soon hires him to take over the show.

I wish Robin Williams were here to bring my stories of money and people to life for you.

If you take a lesson from these chapters and apply it to better your personal financial management, then I've made a contribution to you and we've had success together.

As John Lennon said following the last Beatles concert on a London rooftop: "I'd like to say thank you on behalf of the group and ourselves, and I hope we passed the audition."

INDEX

ABOUT THE AUTHOR

Mitch Fisher was born April 12, 1950, in Los Angeles. He graduated from Inglewood High School in 1968 and earned his bachelor's degree from Claremont McKenna College (known then as Claremont Men's College) in 1972.

He played professional basketball abroad and owned two international businesses. He began his career in financial services in 1974. Mitch has been the acting president of Pacific Sun Financial Corporation since starting the company in 1983.

He is the founding member and former chairman of Saddleback Memorial Hospital Foundation Baby Alumni Club.

Mitch is married with three children and three grandchildren. He lives in Southern California and Kauai.

Made in the USA
Las Vegas, NV
14 January 2022